The Art and Craft *of*
Paper Sculpture

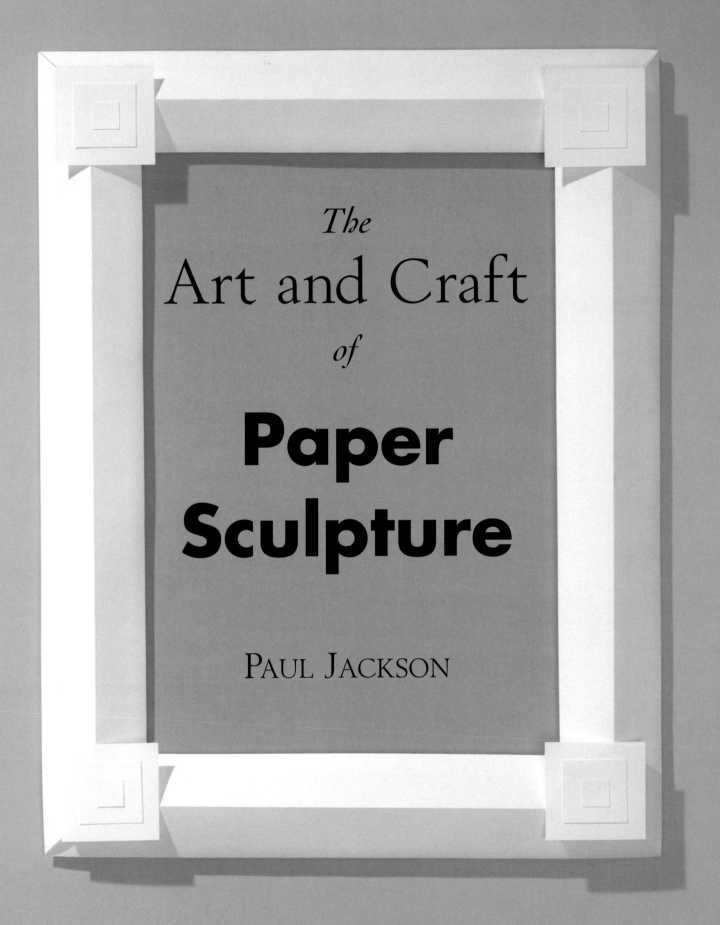

The
Art and Craft
of
Paper
Sculpture

PAUL JACKSON

CHILTON BOOK COMPANY
Radnor, Pennsylvania

A QUARTO BOOK

Copyright © 1996 Quarto Inc.

Reprinted in 1996

ISBN 0−8019−8874−8

A CIP record for this book is available from
the Library of Congress

This book was designed and produced by
Quarto Publishing plc.
The Old Brewery · 6 Blundell Street · London N7 9BH

SENIOR ART EDITOR Clare Baggaley
DESIGNER Debbie Mole
PHOTOGRAPHERS Laura Wickenden, Paul Forrester,
Chas Wilder
ILLUSTRATOR Neil Ballpit
SENIOR EDITORS Gerrie Purcell, Michelle Pickering
EDITOR Mary Senechal
PICTURE RESEARCH MANAGER Giulia Hetherington
PICTURE RESEARCHER Susannah Jayes
ART DIRECTOR Moira Clinch
EDITORIAL DIRECTOR Mark Dartford

Typset in Great Britain by
Type Technique · 121A Cleveland Street · London W1P 5PN
Manufactured by Regent Publishing
Services Ltd. · Hong Kong
Printed in Singapore by Star Standard Industries Pte. Ltd

Using templates

There are two ways to enlarge the templates.
1. Enlarge them on a photocopier to the correct size.
(E.g. original template at 50% size should be
photocopied at 200% to be full size.) Then cut out
the templates, draw around them onto a sheet of
cardboard or stiff paper and then cut out the shape.

2. Draw a grid of squares over the templates. Draw
another grid of squares, proportionately larger, onto
a sheet of cardboard. Then copy the templates onto
the cardboard or stiff paper, using the grid on the
original template as a guide.

How to use
the information boxes

Tools and Materials: These boxes give you a list
of the tools you will need and the amounts and sizes
of paper or cardboard required for each project.

Pieces to Cut: These boxes give you precise
measurements of the pieces to be cut from the
template shapes and additional pieces which do not
require templates.

Note The measurements for the sizes of cardboard
or paper the shapes are to be cut from have been
rounded up to the nearest $1/4$ in ($1/2$ cm) to simplify.
The measurements for the individual pieces are as
precise as possible to ensure a good final result.

Safety Note

Always take care when using sharp blades. For the
correct and safe way to cut cardboard and paper see
the *how to cut* section on page 15.

Note The lines and markings drawn on the pieces in
the step-by-step photography have been drawn in
dark pen to make them clear to follow. Your pencil
markings should be light and easy to erase.

Contents

Introduction

What is paper sculpture?

No two papercraft enthusiasts would give exactly the same answer. It has been variously described as relief illustration, drawing with light and shadow, and as a catchall term for forms of paper art that are not paper engineering, origami, or modelmaking. The term paper sculpture means different things to different people.

T his book adopts a wide definition, presenting step-by-step instructions for projects which are in relief and fully three-dimensional, expressive and geometric, decorative and practical, so that everyone will find something of interest to make.

The **Techniques** section describes the basics of paper sculpture, and should be read carefully by beginners. Explanations for the **Projects** frequently refer to the **Techniques**, so be prepared to move to and fro between the sections. Experiment with some of the easy designs before trying more intricate creations.

A step-by-step sequence implies that a project must be made exactly the way it is explained. With papercrafts such as origami and pop-ups, this can be true; but with paper sculpture, it is not. The sequences given here will guide you only as closely as you want. You are encouraged to change the final appearance of a sculpture as much as you like! Most of the projects can be simplified, or made more complex, or be used as the inspiration for a radically different piece of work, so if you feel restrained by copying, please diverge from the instructions. There are many helpful suggestions in the book to help you to do this.

The final **Gallery** section presents a selection of sculptures by professionals, students, and talented amateurs. This is the first time that a collection of this breadth and quality has been published in one volume, so I hope that you find it inspirational. Paper sculpture in all its forms is becoming popular again after a couple of quiet decades, and the **Gallery** reflects this new awakening. It is increasingly used as a form of illustration, taught in schools and colleges, and utilized to decorate the home. This seems to be more than just a fashion: paper sculpture deserves its reputation alongside other papercrafts and is here to stay.

I hope that you enjoy the book, and will spend many rewarding hours with this wonderful craft.

Paul Jackson

BASIC
TECHNIQUES

WHEN LEARNING ANY ART OR
CRAFT, IT IS NECESSARY TO FIRST
UNDERSTAND SOME OF THE BASIC
TECHNIQUES. BY THEMSELVES THEY
MAY SEEM UNINSPIRING, BUT THESE
TECHNIQUES WILL BE BROUGHT TO
LIFE IN THE PROJECTS SECTION THAT
FOLLOWS, WHERE THEY ARE GIVEN
CONTEXT AND MEANING WITHIN
A DESIGN.

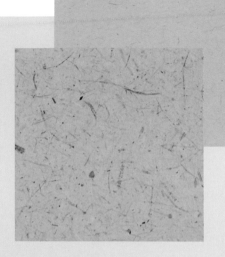

PAPER SCULPTURES SHOULD BE MADE FROM EITHER HEAVY PAPER OR THIN CARDBOARD. MOST ART SUPPLY STORES CARRY A GOOD SELECTION OF BOTH IN A WIDE RANGE OF WEIGHTS, COLORS, AND TEXTURES. CHOOSING WHAT TO BUY CAN BE ALMOST AS MUCH FUN AS MAKING THE SCULPTURE!

PAPER AND BOARDS

Don't be misled by the apparent flimsiness of the large sheets in a store. Smaller offcuts can become surprisingly rigid when creased, cut, bent, glued, and joined to others. So it is often better to buy a weight that is slightly lighter than seems correct. Thicker cardboard may appear to be a safer purchase, but it can be difficult to manipulate and makes a sculpture look stiffer than it should.

Other useful sources of supplies include printing and photocopying businesses which use a variety of papers and boards and may supply what you need, though the size of sheet could be limited. A larger paper or printer company will probably only

deal in bulk orders. But a local paper merchant – listed in the Yellow Pages – could provide booklets of samples from the manufacturers to help you become familiar with different types of paper. They might also be willing to order what you need or advise you where to obtain it.

Remember, whatever the source of your purchase, use boards and papers from a single line for each particular project or for work that is to be shown together. The finishes of different types – matte, glossy, flecked, and so on – often vary, and can look incompatible side-by-side, however suitable they are individually. Avoid "coated" cardboard, that is, white board with a colored surface layer. When it is creased, the coating either flakes off to reveal the white cardboard beneath, or the white becomes visible along the line of the crease. Choose the finest paper and cardboard that you can afford. It will respond better to handling and will not fade or yellow with age, unless exposed to direct sunlight for long periods. Cardboard with a high rag content, or which is pH neutral, is the highest quality.

Correct storage is also important – and often overlooked. Do not keep paper and cardboard rolled up, because fibers acquire a tendency to stay coiled when you want to unwind them. They will flatten if you roll

them inside out, but this often leaves unsightly buckle marks across the sheet. So store your cardboard and paper flat. The easiest way to do this is to place them between large sheets of thick cardboard, tucked under a bed or in a similar out-of-the-way place. An artist's portfolio – the rigid type without plastic sleeves – gives even better protection. For the serious enthusiast, though, nothing can quite compare with the convenience of a flat filing cabinet. They are quite expensive when new, but you may find a bargain at a secondhand office equipment store.

EQUIPMENT

ONE OF THE ATTRACTIONS OF PAPER SCULPTURE IS THAT YOU CAN DO IT WITH EASILY AVAILABLE, INEXPENSIVE EQUIPMENT. A LOCAL STATIONERY STORE WILL CARRY MOST OF THE ITEMS YOU NEED. THERE ARE TWO ADDITIONAL SPECIALIST TOOLS THAT YOU WILL FIND VERY USEFUL: A CUTTING KNIFE WITH A FINELY POINTED BLADE AND A SELF-HEALING CUTTING MAT.

Equipment List

self-healing cutting mat ✪ craft knife ✪ foamboard ✪ sharply pointed blades ✪ pair of compasses ✪ hard pencil ✪ eraser ✪ protractor ✪ ruler ✪ two-sided tape ✪ masking tape ✪ paper glue ✪ thread ✪ fiber-tip pens ✪ needle or hole punch ✪ scissors ✪ tracing paper ✪ paper fasteners ✪ 'M'-shaped straight edge ✪

FOAMBOARD

Foamboard, or foamcore, is a sheet of plastic foam sandwiched between two pieces of cardboard. It is immensely rigid yet very light, and serves to support relief elements at different heights above the background. Corrugated cardboard is a suitable substitute, but foamboard is sturdier and easier to cut. You can buy it in different thickness from art or craft supply stores. It is expensive, but one sheet will make supports for many sculptures.

CRAFT KNIFE

A slim, craft knife with a rounded end to the handle and a long, narrow blade cuts sharply and cleanly. This type is preferable to a heavy-duty craft knife with a cylindrical handle or one with wedge-shaped, retractable, snap-off blades. The slim, rounded handle is easy to manipulate and useful for curling paper (see the *Rose*, p.50). You can buy the knife complete, but a more practical alternative, such as the X-Acto knife, has replaceable and interchangeable blades, so that you can choose the most efficient and comfortable combinations for you. Your local craft or art store will carry a selection and can suggest the most suitable blades – identified by number.

SELF-HEALING CUTTING MAT

These mats have the useful property of sealing any knife cut so that, unlike wood or board, they never become pitted. This means that your blade will never slip through the cardboard into an existing cut in your work surface and veer annoyingly off course. Using a self-healing mat, a cut will always go where you put it. Although it may seem expensive, such a mat should remain in good condition for many years, and once used, it tends to become indispensable.

TECHNIQUES

Paper consists of vegetable fibers. During the manufacturing process, the half-formed paper sheet is vibrated on a moving belt so that the

The nature of paper

fibers line up in parallel. This gives paper greater flexibility along the line of the fibers than across them. When you bend or tear paper (or cardboard), the influence of the parallel fibers – called "the grain" – is important.

TESTING FOR THE GRAIN

Here is a simple method of finding the direction of the grain.

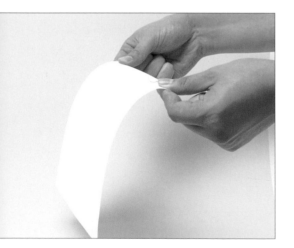

2 Rotate the sheet 90° and hold it in the same way by a neighboring edge. This time the paper is stiffer and tends to curve less, because the fibers are *perpendicular* to the held edge.

1 Hold the paper firmly along one edge, and allow it to bend gracefully under its own weight. If the fibers are *parallel* to the held edge, the sheet will curve a lot, as this one does.

ROLLING

Choosing the correct direction makes rolling more effective.

1 Rolling is easier with the grain – when the fibers lie along the length of the tube.

TEARING

You can control the character of a torn edge by tearing with or across the fibers.

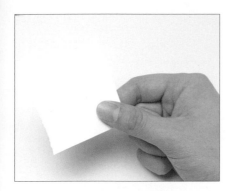

1 The torn edge at the top of the sheet is more jagged than that on the left. It was made by tearing across the grain; the straighter edge follows the direction of the fibers.

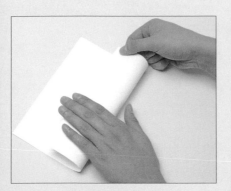

2 It can be very difficult to roll against the grain – when the fibers lie across the tube. This may even buckle the paper.

How to cut

It is vital to learn a few simple rules before bringing sharp blades and vulnerable fingers into close proximity. The key is to always put your free hand out of the way of the blade.

CUTTING AGAINST A STRAIGHT EDGE

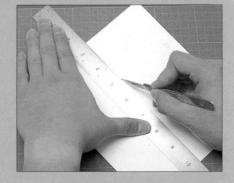

1 Incorrect! It is tempting to place your thumb across the ruler, because this is a natural position, but it puts the tip of your thumb in the path of the blade.

2 Correct! The thumb is pressing against the outside edge of the ruler, well clear of the blade. An M-shaped straight edge would be even safer, but is more unwieldly than a flat ruler.

CUTTING FREEHAND

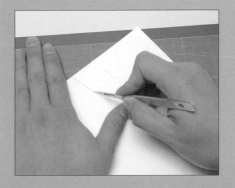

1 Incorrect! The hand that holds the cardboard during cutting should never be even partially below the blade or in line with it.

2 Correct! The steadying hand is safely positioned, well away from the blade.

There are two basic ways to make a straight or curved crease: by cutting partly through the cardboard with a sharp knife (known as "scoring"), or by using the blunt edge

Creasing

(back) of the blade to indent the chosen line. Indenting produces a flexible crease and is usually preferable to scoring, which weakens the cardboard.

SCORING

1 With the point of a blade, cut about halfway through the cardboard along the line of the crease.

2 Bend the cardboard backward along the score.

3 Above, the completed score. However, on coated cardboard, such as this, scoring reveals the white board beneath the color, and the effect is not good. Also, even light scoring reduces the thickness of the cardboard and therefore its strength. It is better to crease by *indenting* (see opposite).

INDENTING

❶ This is the white side of a red-coated sheet similar to that shown in *scoring* (see opposite). To crease, turn the blade upside down, and press it into the cardboard along the line of the crease, against the edge of a ruler or freehand. Make sure that you do not break the surface of the cardboard.

❷ Bend the sheet toward you to form the crease.

❸ Turn the cardboard over to the red side. Compare this crease with the scored edge (opposite). There is no white line, and the sheet remains strong. Note that while scoring is done on the outside surface of the cardboard, indented creasing is done on the inside.

CURVED CREASES

Curved creases differentiate paper sculpture from paper engineering and origami, both of which normally use only straight creases. Utilized well, the technique can create flowing relief forms which look beautiful when carefully lit. To make the creases, use either of the methods described.

Curved creases can be produced in three basic forms: singly; as a series of carefully placed mountain creases; or as a mountain/valley pleat (see p.18). Whatever the pattern, draw the creases on the cardboard first, either freehand or using a mechanical aid such as a pair of compasses.

Bend each crease into shape. Use controlled pressure and take your time – if you are too forceful, the card will buckle.

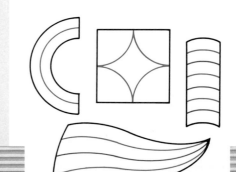

RIGHT *Curved creases occur frequently in the* Projects *and* Gallery *sections. This is because an edge created by a curved crease looks more natural than a straight edge* *and therefore suits the layered drawing style of relief paper sculptures. Another reason they are used often is that curved creases look beautiful!*

Pleats

Pleating is an easy but effective way to create relief forms. It can also texture a surface by producing patterns of light and shade. Make each crease by *indenting* (see p.17), not scoring, always turning the sheet over to make the crease on the inside.

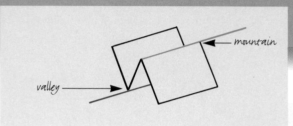

The number of possible pleating patterns is huge and, for the geometrically minded paper sculptor, almost a subject in itself. The key to success is to measure and crease with great accuracy. When designing pleats for a sculpture, such as the fins of the *Fish* (see p.78), take a little time to experiment with the different patterns.

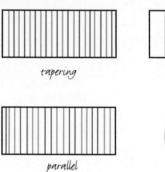

tapering

box

parallel

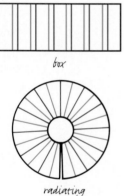

radiating

LEFT *The final form of a pleat is often difficult to guess from the crease pattern, and the play of light can be just as surprising – and beautiful. Take time to explore the varied effects of inward (valley) and outward (mountain) creases, radiating pleats, parallel pleats, tapering pleats and box pleats – to name but a few.*

1 Press each crease firmly and cleanly, working systematically along the line of pleats. The cardboard will often become surprisingly rigid.

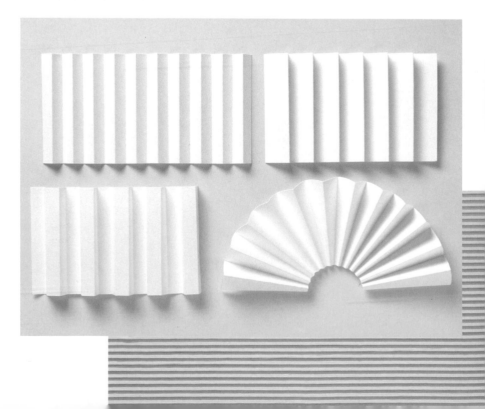

Zigzag pleats

Zigzag pleats are sets of parallel or converging pleats that meet along a central crease to form a V shape. They can take on many guises, such as the eyes on the *Pop-up head* (p.74), and the *Fall leaves* (p.72). They are one of the most useful of all paper sculpture techniques.

Zigzag pleats are hard to make free hand – especially in cardboard – and must be accurately measured and drawn before being creased. The top two examples are conventional zigzag pleats. The bottom two are "crimps," (see p.26) creased first to the inside, then to the outside. The convergence of the V creases at the center crease differentiates them from conventional zigzag pleats.

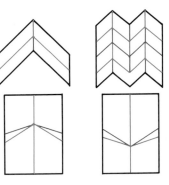

BELOW *The upturned V at the top left can be extended sideways and downward infinite times to create a repeat pattern such as the M-shaped piece at top right. The crimp effect on the lower examples is used to make the Elephant (p.44), and can be combined with the upper two.*

1 To form a zigzag pleat, make all the creases, then squeeze the edges of the sheet together. All the creases will form at once, collapsing the sheet in a concertina-like pattern.

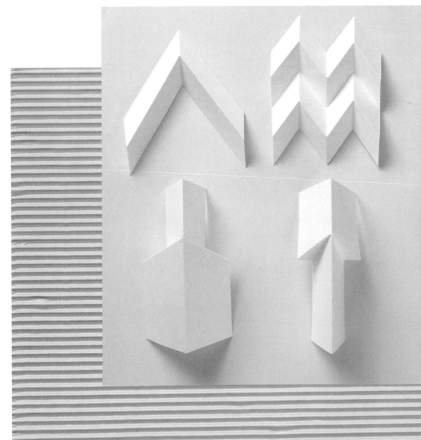

Pop-ups

There is an overlap between the techniques of paper sculpture and of pop-ups, which creates an aesthetic style midway between the two. The cut-and-fold pop-up technique described here can become highly complex, but even basic triangular and step forms can look good and have many uses. The method described here can be used to create rectangular pop- ups as well as triangular ones.

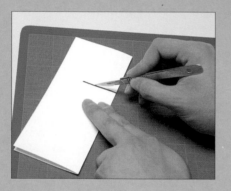

1 Fold a sheet of cardboard in half. Make a cut, as shown, through both layers, ending at the crease.

2 Create a sloping crease from the cut edge, pressing firmly through both layers. If the cardboard is too thick to fold easily then indent the crease first (see p.17).

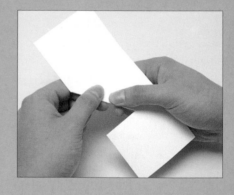

3 Fold the same triangle around to the back of the sheet, so that the crease can flex forward or backward.

4 Unfold the triangle, then open the center crease. The V of the triangular crease can be seen.

5 Hold the sheet slightly bent at the crease, and push up the triangle from the back. Notice that all the creases are valleys, except for the short mountain crease down the center of the triangle.

6 Fold the sheet in half with the triangle forming a pop-up inside. Press it flat to strengthen all the creases. Then unfold it to achieve the final form seen here.

Textured surfaces

The techniques of paper sculpture are more readily associated with form than with texture. Nevertheless, a wonderful range of expressive textures can be created by cutting and lifting the surface of the cardboard. The possibilities of texture are well worth the exploration.

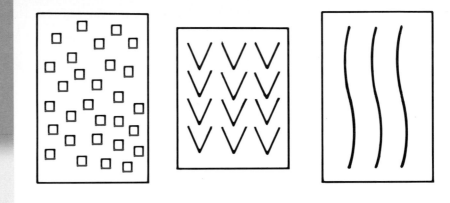

Texture patterns can be drawn precisely, or improvised more randomly. If symmetry is important, measure the position of the cuts and mark a grid on the back of the sheet. Consider the density of the texture and the spacing of the cuts.

1 Curl the tip of each triangle upward, making sure that all are equally curved. Place an identical piece of uncut cardboard beneath the sheet to fill the holes made by the curls.

ABOVE *Texturing will only be visible if it creates a pattern of light and shadow. The same effect can look astonishingly different depending upon the direction from which it is lit. So think about where you will place your light before cutting.*

Tabbing

Tabs are used to join the edge of one component to the surface of another. They come in two forms: integral and invisible. Whichever form is used it is important to be precise with the marking and cutting out of tabs. Of all the paper sculpture techniques, tabbing is the most ingenious and possibly the most satisfying.

INTEGRAL TABS

Integral tabs are made from the same piece of cardboard as the main shape. The need for tabs must be anticipated before the shape is cut, so that the tabs can be included.

Draw the shape, including two tabs on the bottom edge. The tabs should be about ¼in (6mm) wide – neither too wide nor too narrow.

1 Mark the places where the tabs will touch the backing sheet when the vertical cardboard shape is lowered onto it. Make two slits in the backing sheet, the same width as the tabs.

2 Push the tabs through the slits, being careful not to tear the openings or buckle the backing sheet. A tight fit will look and function best.

3 Turn the sheet over and hold the tabs in position on the underside with adhesive tape or glue.

INVISIBLE TABS

It is easy to join a straight edge to a backing sheet, but the challenge is greater when the edge is curved or in a 3-D form of awkward shape. The answer is an invisible tab, made from a separate sheet of cardboard.

Cut out two pieces of cardboard as shown. Bend the circle segment into a cone and glue it into shape.

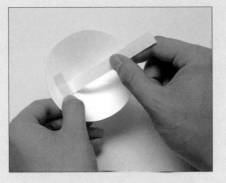

1 Using adhesive tape (or glue), fasten the long tab inside the cone. Its exact position is unimportant, but it would be unwise to put it very close to the edge of the cone.

2 Decide where the cone should sit on the backing sheet. Then make a slit in the sheet as wide as the tab. This should line up approximately with the position of the tab on the cone but there is no need to try and locate it exactly.

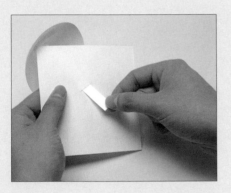

3 Pull the tab through the slit until the cone is held tightly against the backing sheet.

4 Hold the tab securely in place with adhesive tape (or glue).

RIGHT *The finished result. The tab is invisible, allowing the edge of the cone to remain untabbed and perfectly round. With this technique, any volumetric shape can be secured to any other shape, flat or 3-D. A complex form may need two or more tabs to hold it in place.*

Layered relief

Layering paper

is a simple technique derived from collage, and is widely used in paper sculpture. The result is especially dramatic when different colors are layered, as in the *Matisse paper cutout* (p.54), for example. Or a subtle light-and-shadow effect can be achieved with layers of identical paper.

1 Take a square of cardboard and glue a smaller square in the center of it. Check its position for accuracy before the glue sets.

2 Add a further and smaller square on top.

3 Glue a final square into place to complete the layers.

RIGHT *The finished piece relies on light to throw its narrow highlights and shadows into relief. Differently colored layers would create greater impact with less help from light, but would create a flatter, less sculpted surface.*

Blocked relief

Blocked reliefs are similar to *layered reliefs*, except that each of the layers are separated by foamboard supports (see p.12) and appear to "float." They also cast larger shadows. The effect is therefore more striking, and this is an easy way to create visually dynamic reliefs.

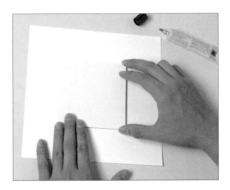  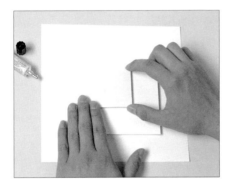

1 Glue a piece of foamboard to the backing sheet. The foamboard must be slightly smaller than its covering layer, so that it will be concealed.

2 Glue a sheet of cardboard to the foamboard, making sure that it overlaps equally on all sides.

3 Add a piece of foamboard, again a little smaller than the following sheet of cardboard.

4 Glue the next sheet of cardboard to its foamboard support. Check for equal overlap all around. Continue in the same way with the final square of foamboard. Glue the last piece of cardboard into position.

RIGHT *Compare the result with the* layered relief *(opposite). To vary the effect, use foamboards of different thicknesses, which will change the width of the shadows. Increase thickness by gluing two pieces of foamboard together if necessary, or use thick cardboard.*

This is the simplest and most versatile way to create a

Crimping

curved form from a flat sheet of cardboard. It is used many times in the *Projects*, such as on the wings of the *Swan* (p56), the petals of the *Rose* (p50) and the head of the *Rooster* (p.82).

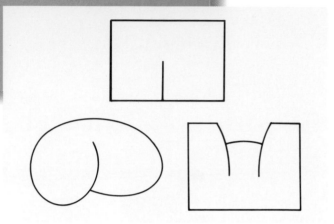

There are three versions of the crimp: along an edge (top), continuing a curved edge (bottom left), and both together (bottom right). The common element is a cut from the edge toward the center of the sheet. The shape of the cut and its position in relation to the edge will dictate the final result.

1 Hold the sheet on either side of the slit, with the back facing you.

2 Overlap the cardboard across the slit and hold the form in place with a piece of adhesive tape. The layers could be glued together instead.

3 Make sure that the cardboard on each side of the cut is equally tensed, so that the layers do not buckle when they are taped or glued together.

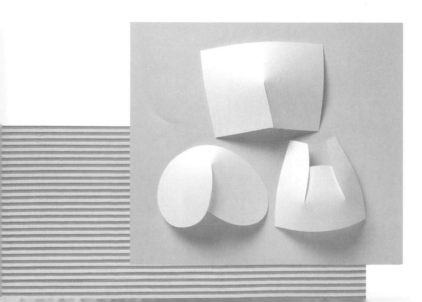

LEFT *The amount of overlap determines how pointed the cone becomes. In most paper sculptures it remains shallow. Many crimps can be created on the same sheet to produce a complex outline. Alternatively, the cut itself can be intricate, as on the Rooster's head (p.82).*

Using light

Lighting is one of the most important considerations in paper sculpture. A relief sculpture owes its impact almost exclusively to the way it is lit. And although light is less vital to more 3-D or to free-standing pieces, it still has the power to make a good piece look superb. Experienced sculptors try to consider the effects of light from the moment they begin a design. There are even those who think of their paper as a means to control light and shadow rather than a way to achieve form. So don't treat lighting as a bonus or optional extra. Use it well and your sculptures will come to life.

Always light a relief sculpture from a single source at the side or above. Front lighting does not create shadows and makes even the most beautiful relief appear flat and uninteresting. Side lighting produces a play of light and shade across the surface of the sculpture and you should consider these effects when designing your sculpture. This is especially important if the sculpture is mostly one color – probably white – because the pattern of light and shade will be more pronounced than any color effect.

Most sculptures will spend part of their time in natural light. So if you are positioning a sculpture on a wall that is lit from one side by day and from another angle at night, make sure that it looks good under both lighting conditions – or consider moving it.

RIGHT *Compare and contrast the play of light and shadow over the surface of the shapes in these two photographs. The forms are the same in both pictures, but the light source was changed from the bottom to the top. The differences in depth of shadow and degree of relief dramatically illustrate the importance of considering the position of your light source.*

DECORATIVE
FRAMES

ALL RELIEF PAPER

SCULPTURES LOOK

GOOD DISPLAYED BEHIND GLASS INSIDE A FRAME. ONCE

BEHIND GLASS, THE SCULPTURE

IS PROTECTED FROM DUST

AND DAMAGE, AND WILL LAST

FOR YEARS.

The frame will need to be a little deeper than one made for a painting, to accommodate the built-up layers of the sculpture. If you do not know of a framer, check the Yellow Pages, or try contacting a local art center. Directories or craft magazines at your public library may also be helpful.

Like most paintings, sculptures will probably also benefit from being housed within a border or "mat" – a piece of thick, colored cardboard –

that separates it from the frame. The mat focuses the eye on the image and helps to relate it to the color of the surrounding wall, and beyond. The frame can then be simple and narrow – and inexpensive – although an ornate frame can also look attractive.

If you do not want to have the sculpture framed under glass, you will need to make a mat for it. Displayed without some framing device, even the most beautiful and detailed relief will look incomplete. In this situation,

a cardboard backing mat fulfills the role of a frame.

So what is the most suitable frame (or mat) to make? It could be plain, decorative, muted, exuberant, curved, collaged, pleated, flat, or multi-layered – there is no single answer, except to create a frame that rounds off the sculpture inside and does not dominate it.

If in doubt, make a frame that is simple, subdued, and not too wide. If it looks too plain, add some subtle decoration, then maybe a little more, as you think you need it. A sensitively designed frame will heighten the impact of any relief sculpture, so it is worth taking time and care to make one that is just right.

The frames explained here show the making of one corner in each case. Construct all the corners in the same way, using a single sheet of cardboard – not separate pieces for each corner. The examples here show some of the main styles of frame, but the possibilities are endless.

Layered frame

This is a simple, flat frame, best used for relief sculptures that are themselves almost flat, such as the *Cloudscape* (p.95)

Tools and Materials

cardboard ✪ knife ✪ ruler ✪ adhesive

1 Glue the frame to the background of the paper sculpture, making sure that there is enough overlap to form a strong bond.

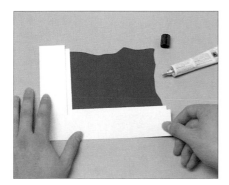

2 Measure and cut another frame which is ¼in (6mm) wider along each edge than the first. Carefully glue it into position, creating a narrow inner "step," and ensuring that all the edges are parallel and the borders equal.

ABOVE *This "double" frame is minimal but attractive, and is suitable for most relief paper sculptures. If it is too plain for your requirements, make the two frames from different colors, or from textured or patterned materials.*

Supported frame

This is a variation of the *layered frame* (p.29). Its extra depth makes it suitable for bulkier sculptures.

Tools and Materials

cardboard ✪ knife ✪ ruler ✪ adhesive ✪ foamboard

1 Glue a foamboard support frame to the background. It must be wide enough to be strong but not to show when the frame is completed.

2 Glue a cardboard frame to the support, hiding it from view.

3 Add another foamboard support to the frame.

LEFT *The shadows cast between the separated layers of the frame create an attractive effect. Be careful not to put too much pressure on the inner and outer edges of the frame, because this can damage them and spoil the straight edges.*

4 Measure and cut another cardboard frame with edges $^{1}/_{4}$in (6mm) wider than the first. Carefully glue it over the base frame in a similar way to Step **2** of the *layered frame* (p.29).

Indented frame

This is a minimal frame that needs good lighting – from the side or the top – to create delicate light and dark lines at the indentations to complement a subtle sculpture.

Tools and Materials

cardboard ✪ knife ✪ straight edge (or ruler) ✪ adhesive

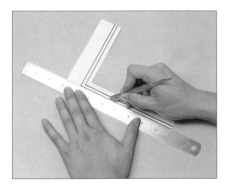

1 Cut out a cardboard frame. Lightly draw two parallel lines around the frame. Using a knife handle and a straight edge, indent the lines with considerable force. Be careful not to overshoot the corners.

2 The lines here are drawn in heavy black for visibility. Your lines should be lightly drawn. Erase the pencil lines and glue the frame securely to the background.

ABOVE *To increase the effect, indent additional lines. You can also use your knife to crosshatch a pattern of indentations, draw curves, write a title, and so on.*

Relief frame

The key to this construction lies in the angle at the corners. It is not 90°, but about 98°, and collapses to 90° when the creases are made. When drawn, therefore, the frame is not a rectangle, but a quadrangle: three of the corners are solid, the fourth is split between the two ends (see diagram below left).

Tools and Materials

cardboard ✪ knife ✪ protractor ✪ straight edge (or ruler)

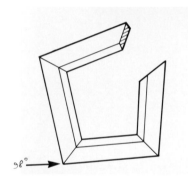

1 Measure the frame as described above, including a glue tab at one end. Draw a line close and parallel to the inner edge. Crease it with an upturned blade. Similarly, crease diagonally across each corner.

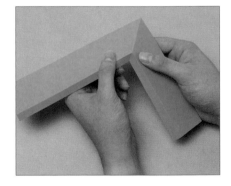

LEFT *The larger the angle at the corners, the deeper the frame will be. For a shallow frame, make the angle only 92°. For a steep incline, increase to 100°. Experiment by creating one corner before tackling a complete frame.*

2 Collapse the creases as shown. The three solid corners will contract to 90°, and the remaining corner, divided between the two ends, will close up to complete the solid frame.

3 Secure the relief frame to the background with a series of tabs (see *invisible tabbing*, p.23).

Scroll frame

If you use colored cardboard then this is a flamboyant frame, but if made in all white it will look more formal – the choice is yours. The effect in either case is truly sculptural, and so echoes the nature of the image it frames.

Tools and Materials

cardboard ✪ knife ✪ adhesive

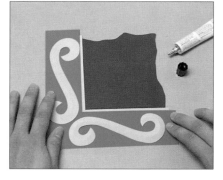

❶ Draw and cut out all of the scrolls. Crease the middle of each form, and bend them to shape.

❷ Apply glue to the ends. Use *integral* or *invisible tabs* (see pp.22–23) if gluing is difficult, or if adhesive may leak into view.

❸ Secure the scrolls to the frame. Note that these are mirror images of each other: they are not identical. Notice also the pale blue inner frame that adds a decorative highlight.

RIGHT *The shapes on the frame could take any form at all, including letters like those on the* Nameplate *(p.46). If your sculpture is subtle, be careful not to overwhelm it with* *a highly ornate frame – such designs can look wonderful, but need to be used with discretion.*

PROJECTS

Having learnt something of the technical terms and skills required for paper sculpture in the previous Techniques section, Projects gives you the experience of applying those techniques in a series of very diverse designs. Gaining experience of these skills is a necessary step on the way to using them expressively, as shown in the concluding Gallery section.

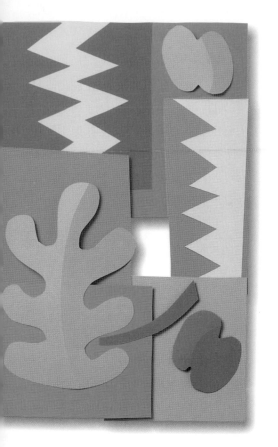

PROJECTS

It is possible to determine some of the basics of paper sculpture by looking at a finished piece, but it is easier to understand how certain effects are achieved when you see an object being constructed step-by-step. This section gives you that information. The projects demonstrate how to put together the techniques introduced in the previous section and how to apply these skills creatively in a wide variety of contexts.

Try not to be over-ambitious at the beginning. Be realistic about how much time and experience you have, and your progress will be pleasingly rapid; setting your sights too high can be dispiriting.

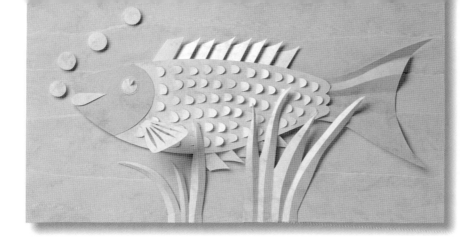

That said, it can be fun to attempt something difficult – provided you truly relish a challenge!

The step-by-step instructions are designed to be easy to follow. The projects will work well if you copy them exactly, but you are encouraged to try your own ideas whenever possible by changing the suggestion to suit yourself. You might want to complicate some aspect, or simplify it; add extra pieces; use different colors; replace a technique; and so on. Paper sculpture is the most creative and least technical of the three-dimensional paper-crafts, so regard the projects as guides – not as models to be slavishly reproduced.

Remember to work neatly, and to concentrate. Regard your first attempt as a "trial" and then make another, final piece.

38

Man in the moon

This is perhaps the easiest project in the book, but nevertheless attractive. Use cardboard with a textured or mottled surface: A smooth or plain sheet can make a simple shape look dull.

Tools and Materials

knife ✪ pair of compasses ✪ thread
✪ needle (or hole punch)
✪ gray marbled cardboard
8x6 in (20x15cm)

Note
Template is 100% size
(This simple shape can also
be drawn freehand, using a pair
of compasses.)

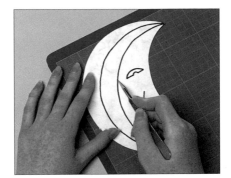

1 Draw the moon, using a pair of compasses to make the curves, and cut it out. Make two curved creases or scores from top to bottom, spacing them equally across the cardboard. Cut two concentric semicircles for the eye. Crease the two short straight creases between the curves of the eye.

2 Bend the two long creases (see p.16) so that one is a valley and the other a mountain (it does not matter which is which). Fold down the flap between the semicircles of the eye to make an opening like a chunky letter C.

RIGHT *Pierce a hole and suspend the moon from a thread. The different facets produced by the curved creases and the folded-down eye will catch the light to create an ever-changing pattern as the crescent revolves in currents of air. Add simple stars, planets, and comets to complete a night sky mobile.*

Decorative or witty sculptures can be made from preprinted papers and boards, or from photocopies. The layering technique

Mona Lisa

used here can be adapted to any image, such as a family photograph or a favorite vacation shot. Make colored photocopies of the picture, or copy it in black and white onto colored papers.

The results are very effective and easy to achieve.

Tools and Materials

knife ✪ adhesive ✪ foamboard
✪ 4 sheets of white cardboard
✪ paper: 1 sheet of each color ~ red,
yellow, green ~ 2 sheets of blue
(Paper size: Use colored paper which is
specially made to fit photocopiers)

Yellow background ⟶

Blue body and frame

Red frame

Green hair

Red head

Red hands

Blue sleeve

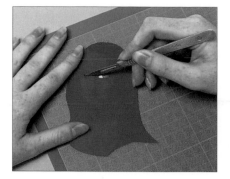

1 Make a photocopy of the Mona Lisa onto three sheets of colored paper: red, yellow, green. Make two copies onto blue paper. Glue the copies onto thin cardboard for stiffness.

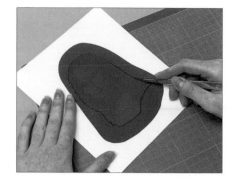

2 Carefully cut out each piece, as shown by the templates on page 41. The yellow photocopy is left complete for the background.

3 Remove the eyes. Glue a small piece of yellow paper behind each eye-hole and draw in the pupils (their gaze will follow you around the room!). Here one eye is completed.

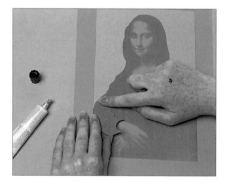

4 The blue piece becomes the body. The body remains joined to the part that forms the blue frame. Glue the separate arm shape to the body at the elbow only, leaving the wrist free.

5 Glue supporting foamboard blocks at regular intervals on the yellow layer. It is better to use lots of small blocks than a few big ones, which would be visible on the finished sculpture.

6 Apply glue to the tops of the blocks. Then carefully lower the blue layer into place, aligning the edges of the frames.

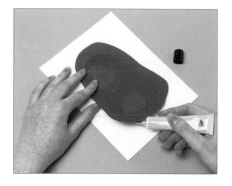

7 Repeating Step **5**, glue foamboard blocks to the blue layer.

8 Glue three further foamboard blocks to the head. Apply adhesive to the tops of the blocks around the frame, and carefully lower the red frame into position.

9 Attach the cutout red shape to the triangle of blocks on the head, checking the alignment all the way around.

RIGHT *The brightly colored, kitsch look of this relief is reminiscent of certain Andy Warhol screenprints. The technique can, of course, be used in more subtle ways. Simply layered black and white photocopies can be stunning. When designing layered reliefs, remember that the surface pattern of the photocopy (or other material) creates its own visual interest, so that the layering can often afford to be correspondingly less complex.*

🔟 Glue the hair into place. To achieve a 3-D effect, press it flat to the neck on your left side, but lift the right-hand side and glue it to a small foamboard block.

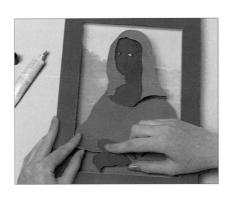

⓫ Stick a supporting block to the blue body where the hands will be positioned. Attach the hands to the top of the block. Lift the loose wrist and glue it under the hands.

Elephant

The *Elephant* is similar to the *Dove* (p.96) because it is derived from origami. Like the *Dove*, it makes repeated use of the *inside crimp* (p.26) to change the direction of the central crease. This crimp technique can be adopted to create other animals, simply by altering the position and angle of the crimps. Experiment by changing the crimps along the elephant's trunk so that it becomes raised instead of lowered as shown here. Choose stiff paper rather than cardboard, which is too thick to allow a crisp angle where the crimps meet the central crease.

Tools and Materials

knife ✪ ruler (or straight edge) ✪ stiff gray paper
12x7½in (30x19cm)
~ *folds in half to become 12x3¾in (30x9.5cm)*

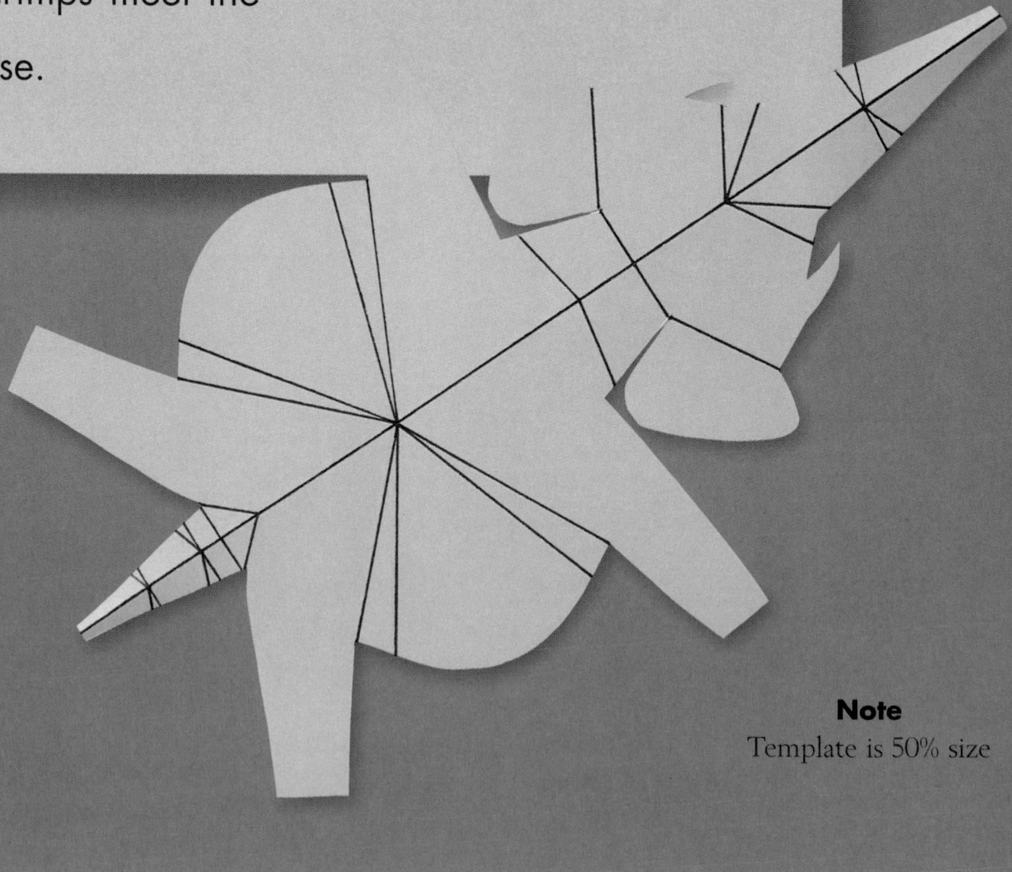

Note
Template is 50% size

1 Score all the creases through both layers, as shown in the template. Begin forming the creases by folding the two pairs of long, shallow crimps that connect the front and back legs with the spine.

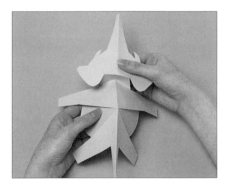

2 Pleat the neck as shown. Look at the Step **3** photograph to locate the position of the head in relation to the body. Adjust the pleat to align them.

ABOVE *The position of the crimps is important if the elephant is to look correctly proportioned, so be prepared for some small errors the first time that you make it. A few minor adjustments should enable you to produce a satisfactory second version without difficulty. If you want more detail, shape the tusks, cut some eyes, and put extra layers on the feet.*

3 Crease the ears. Crimp the trunk twice. Provided its crimps are correctly placed, the trunk will slot behind the tusks, and they will hold it securely in place.

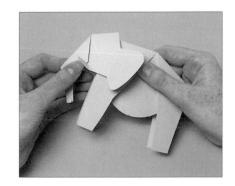

4 Lend a finishing touch of detail by pleating the tip of the trunk, as shown, backward and forward.

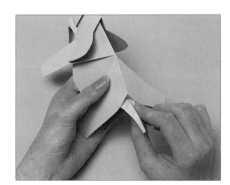

5 Pleat the tail into and back out of the body. Add two small crimps to make the tail point downward, following the line of the body.

Nameplate

The *scoring* **technique** (p.16) produces beautiful raised letters. No calligraphic skills are needed to design them, but it helps to refer to an existing typeface. Choose a style that is neither too slim nor too curved: Thin letters will be too fragile, and it is difficult to position tabs on over-rounded edges. Scroll shapes are perfect for paper sculpture, and are a wonderful embellishment to the letterforms.

Tools and Materials

cardboard: Pale gray, pale blue and mid-blue ✪ knife ✪ adhesive tape ✪ a pair of compasses
(depending on the style of letterforms and scroll-forms made)

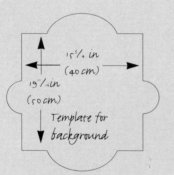

15⅝ in (40 cm)

19¹¹/₁₆ in (50 cm)

Template for background

Pieces to Cut

background: Pale gray cardboard 19¹¹/₁₆x15¾in (50x40cm)
scrolls: *Cut from pale blue cardboard 8x8in (20x20cm)*
large scroll 6in (15cm) long
small scrolls 4.5in (12cm) long
circles 1in (2.5cm) diameter
letterforms: Mid-blue cardboard
cut from a sheet 8x8in (20x20cm)
(uppercase/end letters 4in (10cm)high
lowercase letters 2¾in (7cm) high)

Note
Templates are 50% size

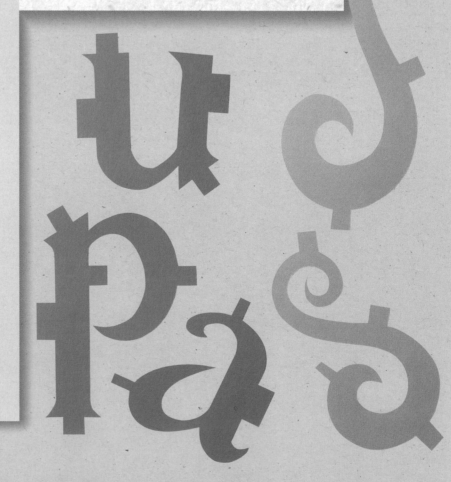

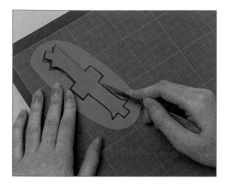

1 Carefully draw each letter shape, including as many tabs as necessary to hold it tightly to the background. Try to position the tabs on straight edges.

2 Score each letter down the center. Notice how the score forks at both ends. Do this neatly.

3 Cut accurately around the scroll decorations and tabs. Score them the same way as the letters.

4 Cut out the background. Arrange the letters and scrolls on it until you are satisfied with the composition. Make a penciled mark on the background to indicate where each tab joins its letter or scroll. Cut small slits in these positions, and slide the tabs through, as shown.

5 Pull each tab through its slit, so that no part is visible from the front. Secure the tabs at the back with the tape.

ABOVE *Use a nameplate on a child's bedroom door, to label an exhibit in a display, as a gift to commemorate an important event, or for any purpose that requires special lettering. Combine the letters with numerals, or with relief images. Notice how the "P" is made with an open loop (see the template illustration) which closes up when the letter is creased. This is because the creasing tightens the curve. So, as can be seen from the template, the curved section must be drawn larger and more open to compensate.*

The typeface shown here is similar to the one used to make

Make up
your own
name

the *Nameplate* project. Use it as reference to design your own. You may wish to widen, shorten or lengthen some of the letter strokes, or add decorative features. Remember you will need to draw tabs onto the letters before cutting.

a b c d e f g
h i j k l m
n o p q r s t
u v w x y z

Rose

The paper-like quality of petals makes many flowers ideal subjects for the paper sculptor. The main problem is how to bend a flat sheet of paper into the delicate curves of a petal so that it does not look stiff. This is achieved by pulling the edge of each petal around a craft knife handle with considerable force, as though trying to stretch the paper. With a little practice, this will create a 3-D effect that is surprisingly beautiful, and perfect for depicting petals.

Tools and Materials

knife ✪ adhesive ✪ two-sided tape
✪ 2 sheets white paper
8½x11in i.e. ALS size (22x28cm)

Pieces to Cut

4 largest petals can be cut from
a sheet 6x7in (15x18cm),
~ *each petal 2⁹⁄₁₆x2¾in (6.5x7cm)*

4 second largest petals can be cut
from a sheet 4¾x5in (12x13cm),
~ *each petal 2x2⅜in (5x6cm)*

4 second smallest petals
can be cut from a sheet
3½x4in (9x11cm),
~ *each petal 1½x1¹³⁄₁₆in (4x4.6cm)*

4 smallest petals can be cut from
a sheet 2⅜x4in (6x10cm),
~ *each petal 1⅝x1in (4.2x2.5cm)*

2 leaves can be cut from a sheet
4½x3in (11x8cm),
~ *each leaf 2³⁄₁₆x3⅛in (5.5x8cm)*

center section 2⅞ (7.3cm)
max. diameter

5 circles, diameters 1½in (3.8cm),
1¼in (3cm), 1¹⁄₁₆in (2.6cm),
⅞in (2.3cm), ¾in (2cm)

Note

Templates are 100% size

Center section

Largest petal
(cut 4)

smallest
petal
(cut 4)

second smallest petal
(cut 4)

Leaf (cut 2)

second largest petal
(cut 4)

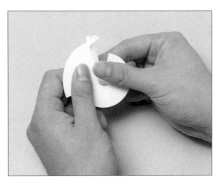

1 Carefully begin to coil up the center section, curling it very tightly around the midpoint.

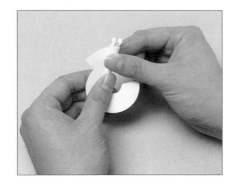

2 Continue winding, taking time to ensure that the spiral is neat and tight.

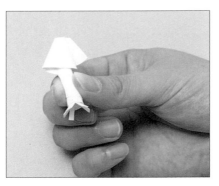

3 When rolling is complete, you will have created a looser coil around the top that resembles a lampshade. Glue the center tube firmly shut and splay out the tabs at the bottom.

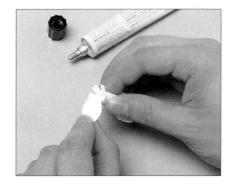

4 Apply adhesive to the smallest circle piece and join it to the underside of the splayed tabs.

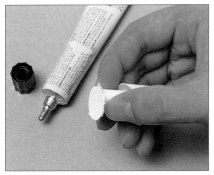

5 This is the result. If the coil begins to unwind, secure it with some more glue.

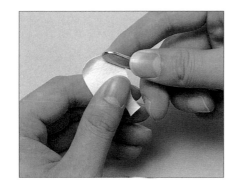

6 Use the handle of a craft knife (or similar rounded edge) to pull and curve one of the smallest set of petals. Curl the entire rim, except for the tabs.

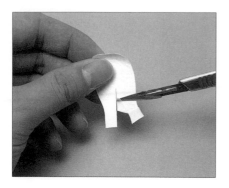

7 Remove the backing strip from a tiny piece of two-sided tape and apply it to the base of the petal, as shown. Note the cut to the left of the tape.

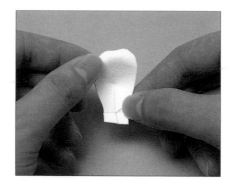

8 Overlap the cardboard across the cut, forming a convex point in the center of the petal. Note the curve to the edge, created in Step **6**.

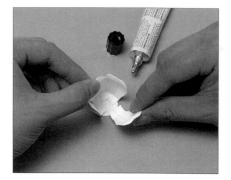

9 Repeat Steps **6** to **8** with three companion petals, and glue them around the edge of the remaining smallest circle.

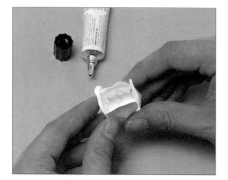

10 The completed unit. If the petals lie a little unevenly this will look more natural. Do not try to neaten them – nature is never so precise!

11 Repeat Steps **6** to **8** with the next-sized set of petals. The result is the same, but larger.

12 Again, apply a tiny piece of two-sided tape alongside the cut at the base before overlapping to shape the petal.

13 As before, glue four completed petals to the smallest remaining circle, avoiding an over-perfect arrangement as this may look "unnatural."

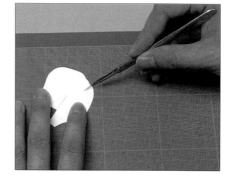

14 With the next size of petal, use the blunt back of the blade to impress a pattern of veins into the paper. Do not break the surface.

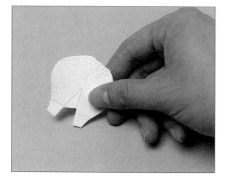

15 This is the result. The effect is best with a large number of veins.

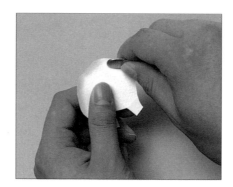

16 As before, pull the edge of the petal against a craft knife handle to curl the rim.

17 Again glue four completed petals to the smallest remaining circle.

18 Impress veins into the largest set of petals.

19 Complete each petal as before, and glue them in the same way to the remaining circle.

20 Impress veins into the two leaves, using an upturned blade. Curl the edge of each leaf as you did the petals, but also between the veins to create a quilted effect.

21 The rose can now be assembled. Glue the circle base of the second largest ring of petals into the middle of the biggest unit.

22 Repeat to attach the next-sized ring of petals.

23 Glue the smallest ring of petals into the center. You may need to adjust the arrangement of individual petals to achieve a natural effect.

24 Add the coiled section, making sure that, visually, it sits in the center of the bloom, and not to one side.

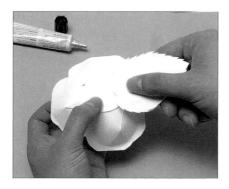

25 Turn the rose over. Glue the leaves firmly to the base, so that they cannot easily be dislodged.

ABOVE *Designing flowers such as the Rose is relatively simple. Just take a real flower – and pull it apart! Copy the shapes of the petals, stamen, and other parts onto cardboard and reassemble them in a perfect imitation of the original. Use the technique of curling the edge wherever appropriate to help shape the petals. Countless flowers can be created this way, each as fine as the Rose.*

Matisse paper cutout

The paper cutouts created by the French artist Henri Matisse (1869–1954) are among the most instantly recognizable and popular images of the 20th century, and translate well into paper sculpture. The layering of the colored cardboard to produce highlights and shadows mimics the advancing and receding effects achieved by Matisse through his masterful use of color, tone, and subtle composition.

Tools and Materials

knife ✪ adhesive ✪ foamboard ✪ colored cardboard: orange, yellow, pale blue, red, green all 12x6in (30x15cm)

Pieces to Cut

orange rectangle
6x12in (15x30cm)

orange rectangle
10x5in (25x12.5cm)

yellow square
10x10in (25x25cm)

pale blue rectangle
12x6in (30x15cm)

red square
10x10in (25x25cm)
(to be cut down the center in a zigzag line to make two pieces)

green rectangle
12x6in (30x15cm)

Note
Templates are 50% size

1 Cut out all the pieces. Glue the first four pieces (yellow, orange and the two red pieces) to the background as shown. Be sure to misalign the pieces around the perimeter to create a casual stepped effect.

2 Apply glue to four foamboard blocks and add them to the background. The upper two are shallower than the lower pair. If you only have one thickness of foamboard on hand, double it to achieve a higher support.

3 Begin gluing colored pieces to the foamboard, starting with the shallower blocks.

4 Continue gluing the pieces to the supports. Remember that it is not important to keep the edges of the design neat.

5 Score the stylized plants and fruit to create light and shadow effects, then glue them to the design. Position them with care, so that the composition is balanced.

RIGHT *The technique of layering on foamboard supports, and scoring some pieces to increase the relief effect, can be applied to any collage. Some of the Cubist collages created by Pablo Picasso and Georges Braque, or the geometric abstracts of Piet Mondrian, would make fine relief sculptures. It is usually better, however, to "interpret" a favorite work than to copy it, so that it takes on its own qualities in terms of paper sculpture.*

Swan

The combination of a graceful shape, white cardboard to maximize light effects, and delicate scoring to show the curve of the wings, makes the swan an irresistible subject.

The construction technique can be adapted to create cygnets, ducks, geese, and any nesting bird, just by changing the proportions. To use the design in a relief – perhaps a pond scene – simply cut the free-standing swan in half. A little extra scoring may be necessary down the neck and along the tail.

Tools and Materials

knife ✪ adhesive tape ✪ yellow and black fiber-tip pens ✪ white cardboard 7x16in (18x40cm) ~ *folds in half to become 7x8in (18x20cm)*

1 Fold the cardboard in half to make a double thickness, then cut out the shape through both layers. Note that the center crease lies between the layers, across the top of the head. Be especially careful to make flowing cuts along the neck.

When unfolded your cut out shape should look like this.

Note
Template is 50% size

2 Cut through both layers along a curved line that follows the bottom edge of the wings.

3 With the back of the blade, make several creases from the cut created in Step **2** to the tip of the wing feathers. Pleat the creases, beginning with a valley at the top.

4 Crimp each wing (see *crimping*, p.26), slightly overlapping the bottom edge with the cardboard beneath to create a very shallow cone, the tapered point of which is at the end of the wing cut. Hold the crimp in place with a tiny piece of adhesive tape.

5 Place a dab of glue between the two layers of the beak, and glue to form a solid double thickness.

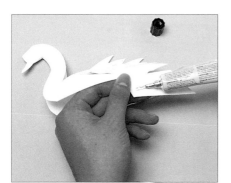

6 Fold the two halves of the tail inside the swan. Glue them together along the top edge only, so that the bottom edges can separate and hold the swan upright.

ABOVE *Add the beak and eye markings with fiber-tip pens. You can use colored cardboard to achieve such finishing touches – and purists might insist on it. But the markings here are so delicate that they would be difficult to make from cardboard, so pens are a prudent choice.*

Collapsible cityscape

Tools and Materials

knife ✪ adhesive ✪ ruler
✪ cardboard
light gray cardboard 14¹⁵⁄₁₆ x 5¹⁵⁄₁₆ in
(38x15cm) *(main piece A)*
white cardboard 8¹¹⁄₁₆ x 5¹⁵⁄₁₆ in
(22x15cm) *(main piece B)*
light gray 4¾ x 5¹⁵⁄₁₆ in (12x15cm)
light brown 4¾ x 5¹⁵⁄₁₆ in (12x15cm)
darker gray 2¾ x 5¹⁵⁄₁₆ in (7x15cm)

Pieces to Cut

light brown rectangle
¹⁵⁄₁₆ x 2¼ in (2.3x5.7cm)
light brown rectangle
¾ x 2¼ in (1.8x5.7cm)
light brown: can all be cut from a
sheet 5¹⁵⁄₁₆ x 7¾ in (15x12cm)
individual sizes of pieces:
(letters marked on template pieces)
A: 2⅜ x 1 in (6x2.5cm)
B: 2½ x 1¹³⁄₁₆ in (6.5x3cm)
C: 4⅜ x 1½ in (11x4cm)
D: 2³⁄₁₆ x ¾ in (5.5x2cm)
E: 3³⁄₁₆ x 1³⁄₁₆ in (8x2cm)
darker gray: can all be cut from a
sheet 6 x 2¾ in (15x7cm)
individual sizes of pieces:
(letters marked on template pieces)
F: 2¼ x 1⁵⁄₁₆ in (5.7x3.4cm)
G: 2 x ¹³⁄₁₆ in (5x2cm)
H: 2½ x 1¹⁄₁₆ in (6.3x1.8cm)
I: 2³⁄₁₆ x 1⅛ in (5.5x2.8cm)
smaller pieces:
Light gray: J: 7¾ x 5¹⁵⁄₁₆ in (12x15cm)

This seemingly intricate construction is based on just two pieces of cardboard. The key to its success is the precise location of the slits and creases, so that all parts interlock and the structure collapses flat. It can be mailed like a card and erected for display when opened. Although this is a pop-up, the free-standing effect creates a form that is truly sculptural.

Note
Templates
Main pieces A and B
are at 50%

Templates A – J
are at 100%

Main piece B

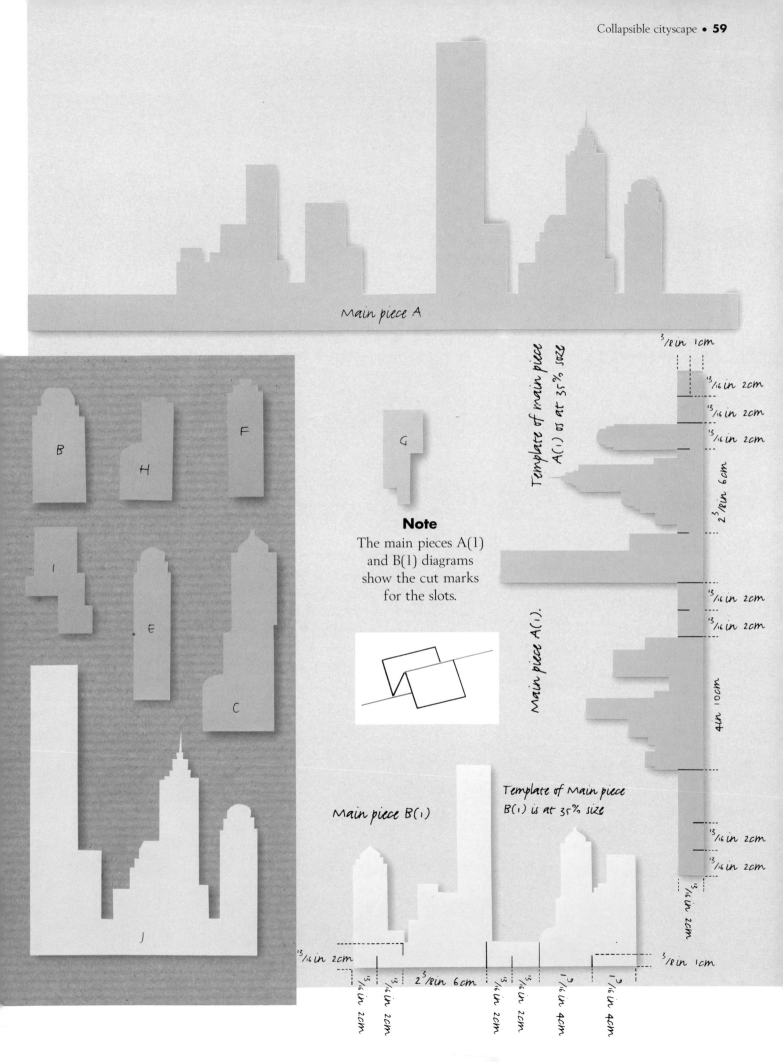

Main piece A

Template of main piece A(1) is at 35% size

$^{3}/_{8}$ in 1cm

$^{13}/_{16}$ in 2cm

$^{13}/_{16}$ in 2cm

$^{13}/_{16}$ in 2cm

$2^{3}/_{8}$ in 6cm

G

Note
The main pieces A(1)
and B(1) diagrams
show the cut marks
for the slots.

Main piece A(1).

$^{13}/_{16}$ in 2cm

$^{13}/_{16}$ in 2cm

4 in 10cm

$^{13}/_{16}$ in 2cm

$^{13}/_{16}$ in 2cm

Template of Main piece
B(1) is at 35% size

Main piece B(1)

$^{3}/_{8}$ in 1cm

$^{13}/_{16}$ in 2cm

$^{13}/_{16}$ in 2cm

$^{13}/_{16}$ in 2cm

$2^{3}/_{8}$ in 6cm

$^{13}/_{16}$ in 2cm

$^{13}/_{16}$ in 2cm

$1^{9}/_{16}$ in 4cm

$1^{9}/_{16}$ in 4cm

B

H

F

I

E

C

J

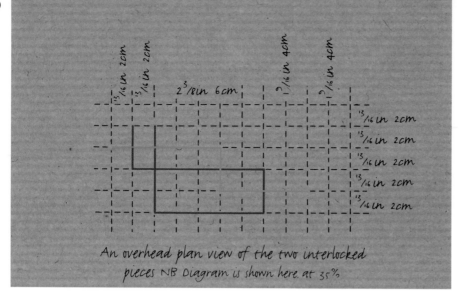

¹³/16 in 2cm

¹³/16 in 2cm

2 ³/8in 6cm

¹/16 in 4cm

⁹/16 in 4cm

¹³/16 in 2cm
¹³/16 in 2cm
¹³/16 in 2cm
¹³/16 in 2cm
¹³/16 in 2cm

An overhead plan view of the two interlocked
pieces NB Diagram is shown here at 35%

1 Cut out both the largest pieces and all the smaller ones.

2 Glue the smaller pieces to the large ones to create the effect of overlapping buildings. Follow this example, or improvise your own pattern.

3 Using a sharp blade, cut out tiny squares in a random grid pattern to create windows. You may want to pencil a grid on the back of the piece as a guide. Do not overdo the effect, or you will lessen its visual impact and weaken the cardboard.

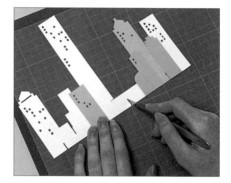

4 Follow the measurements shown on the drawings and make vertical slots in the main pieces, as shown. The measurements must be precise, so check and recheck them before cutting.

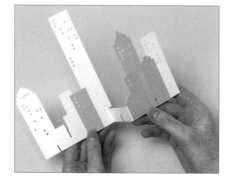

5 With equal care, measure the position of the creases, following the indications in the drawings.

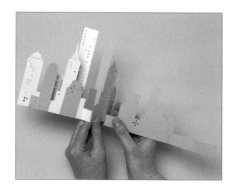

6 Carefully interlock the two main pieces by sliding a slit on one into the corresponding slit on the other. There is no best sequence for this, but it is easy to do.

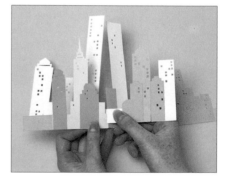

7 Continue to engage the slits in whatever sequence seems appropriate, keeping to the pattern in the diagram shown above.

8 The final pair of slits are the trickiest to join. Hold the sculpture firmly with one hand and use finger and thumb to slot the two pieces together. You may need to ease the previous slits apart slightly to help you.

ABOVE *From above, the cityscape is revealed as a series of connected rectangular boxes. You can form any pattern of boxes to create differently faceted cityscapes, from the simple to the fantastically complex. The technique can be adapted from cityscapes to any* *structure of your imagination. The only imperatives are strict measurement of the slits and creases and the creation of a solid base – if you cut the silhouette too close to the ground, the structure will be weakened.*

Masks are inexpensive, easy to make, and perfect for fancy dress parties or plays. They can cover the entire head, or just the face or eyes.

Mask

Some are made for display only. The basic problem when designing any mask is bending the cardboard around the curves of the face. This is done by connecting the left and right halves of each main piece by a series of tabs which form a curved edge down the forehead, nose, and chin.

Tools and Materials

knife ✪ straight edge (or ruler)
✪ two-sided tape (or glue) ✪ cardboard
Flesh-colored cardboard 18x18in
(45x45cm)

~ individual flesh pieces:
face 12½x12½in (31x31cm)
nose 6x6¼in (15x16cm),
straps 10½x2in (27x5cm) – cut 2
Gray cardboard 20x14in (50x35cm)

~ individual hair pieces:
beard 16x12in (40x30cm),
mustache 7x5in (18x14cm),
eyebrow 4x1½in (10x4cm)
– cut 2

Nose

Mustache

Note
Templates are 50% size

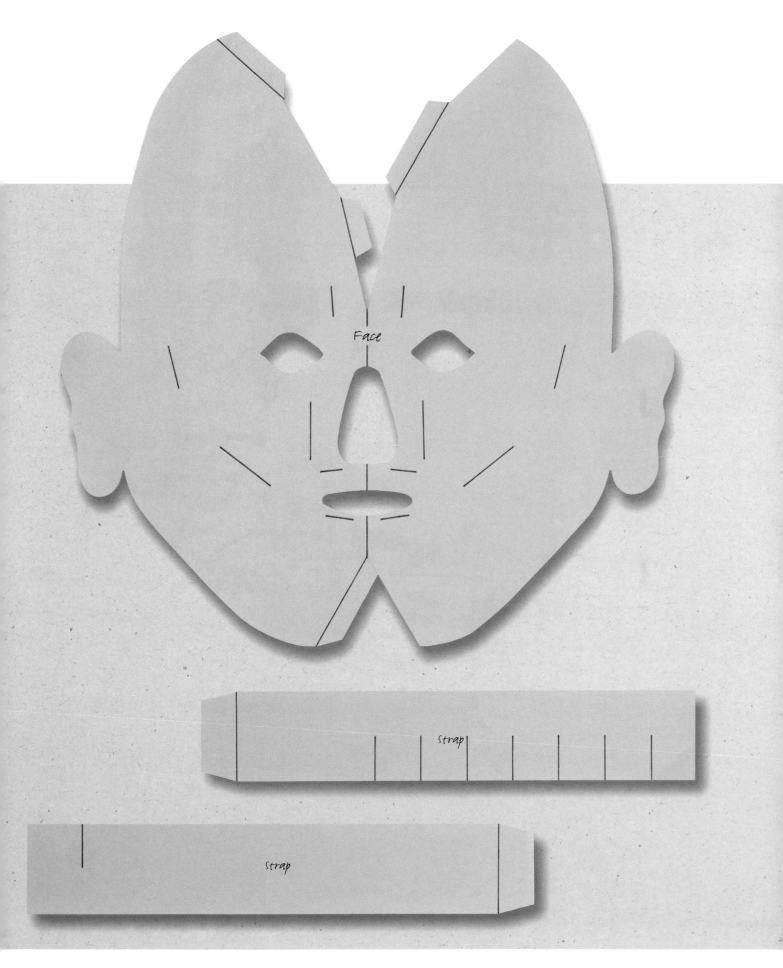

Face

Strap

Strap

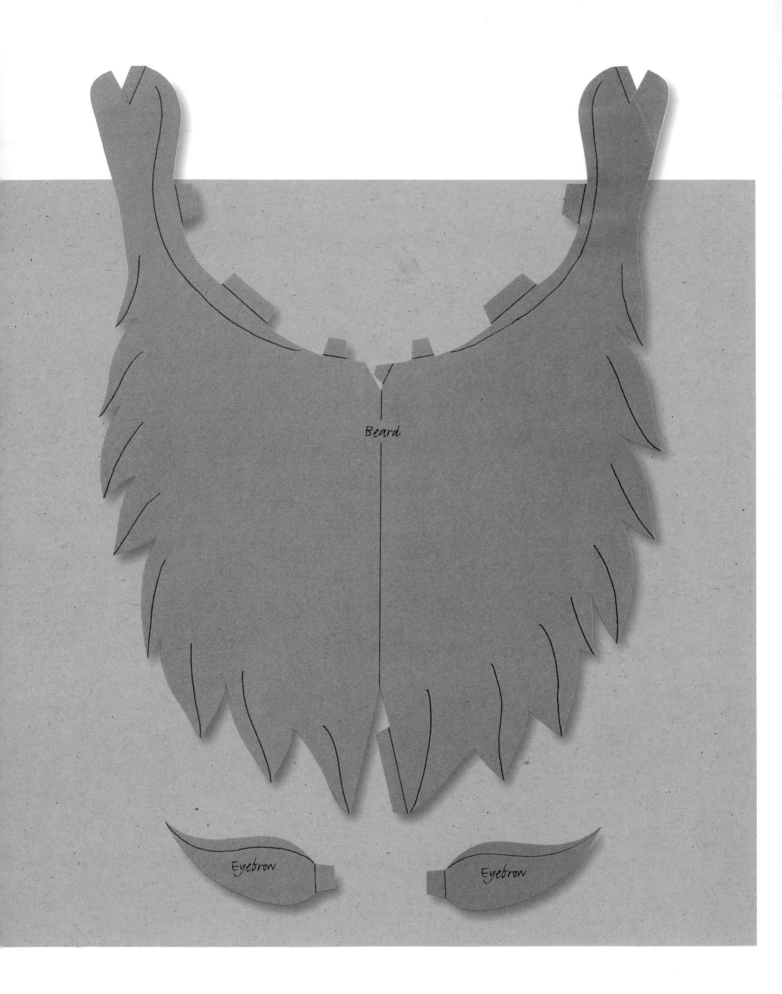

1 Draw all the slots on the face in a symmetrical pattern. Crease across the base of all the tabs around the edge, and crease down the center of the face.

2 Apply two-sided tape to all the tabs at the chin and forehead (glue can be used, but is less effective). Peel the protective backing from the tape.

3 Interlace the tabs to join the two sections of chin and forehead. If this is done accurately, the face will fold flat in half.

4 Using the back of a pointed blade, make short curved creases around the edge of the beard. Pinch the creases and the ends to create a relief effect of straggly hair. Crease the base of all of the beard tabs.

5 Crimp the chin (see *crimping*, p.26) and secure it with two-sided tape. Repeat with the tab at the base of the beard, and again at the ears. Make a crease down the center, so that the beard can fold flat.

6 Score along the top of the cheeks, and insert the beard tabs into the face. This is when you will find that taking care when measuring and double-checking the position of the tabs before cutting out the cardboard will pay off.

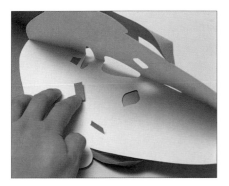

7 Pull the tabs through the face so that they are not visible from the front. Press them flat and secure them with two-sided tape.

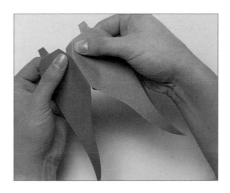

8 Crease and unfold the center of the mustache. Apply two-sided tape to the central tab.

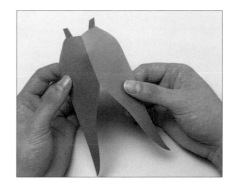

9 Overlap the tab across the middle, so that the top edge of the mustache becomes 3-D.

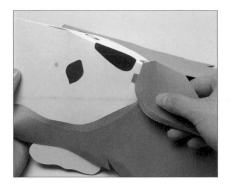

10 Score near the outer edges of the mustache to give it some fullness. Then insert the tabs into the slits in the upper lip, and use two-sided tape to hold them in place.

11 Apply two-sided tape to the tabs at the top of the nose and begin interweaving them to close the edge.

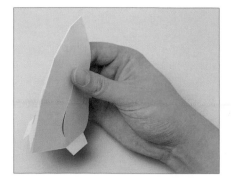

12 When fully interlaced, the nose will fold flat. Note the cut. It can be made beforehand, or now, by cutting through both layers (the tip of the nose is at the top of the photograph).

13 Insert the remaining nose tabs in the face. Fix them into position, as before, using adhesive tape.

14 Crease each eyebrow, as shown. Apply two-sided tape to the front of each tab.

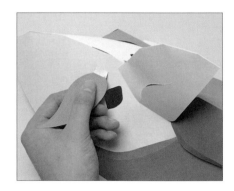

15 Insert each tab through the slots in the face. Note that the protective backing strip is still attached to the tape. Remove it to secure the tabs when the eyebrows are in position.

16 Apply two-sided tape to the end of each half of the strap.

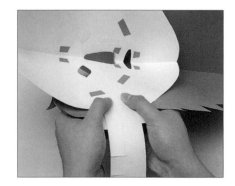

17 Position each of the strap pieces inside the face, approximately level with the ears.

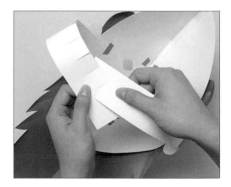

18 The slits are along the top edge of one strap, and the bottom edge of the other. To wear the mask, adjust for a comfortable fit and interlock the slits.

RIGHT *The mask can be adapted in many ways. Add curly scrolls to the beard to create a Greek god. Put on some hair or eyeglasses. Devise a hat or a pipe.*
If the mask is for display only, close the back of the head with an extra piece of cardboard and the top with hair or a hat, and support the sculpture on an invisible central pillar.

Twist-out star

This spectacular decoration is made by repeating a simple technique in a concentric pattern. The cuts and short connecting creases must be aligned precisely to ensure that the arms of the star are sufficiently strong. So follow the drawing sequence exactly before cutting and creasing the cardboard. The final twisting must also be copied with care.

Tools and Materials

knife ✪ straight edge (or ruler)
✪ hole punch (or needle) ✪ cardboard
*(The cardboard can be plain white
or colored on one side.)*

Note
Diagrams are 80% size

❶ Cut out the shape of the star so that the points are not too sharp. As shown, draw the four principal lines of symmetry.

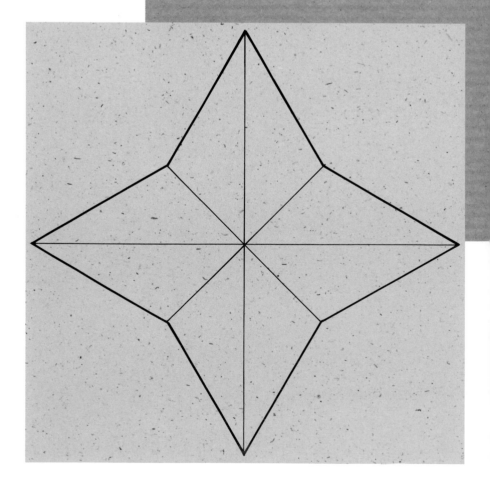

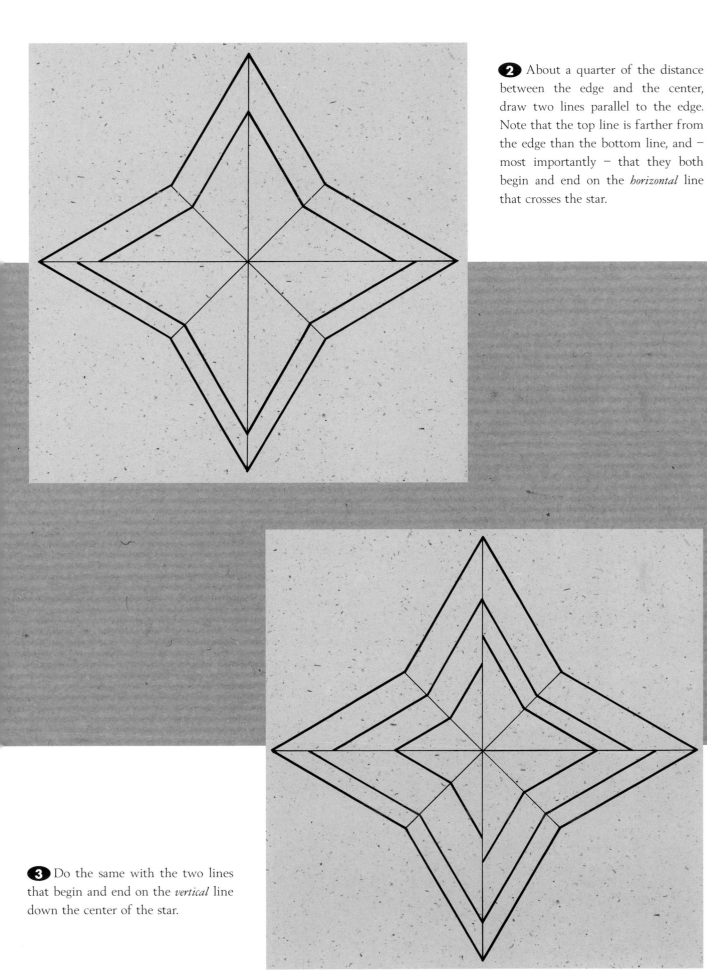

2 About a quarter of the distance between the edge and the center, draw two lines parallel to the edge. Note that the top line is farther from the edge than the bottom line, and − most importantly − that they both begin and end on the *horizontal* line that crosses the star.

3 Do the same with the two lines that begin and end on the *vertical* line down the center of the star.

4 Repeat the Step **2** pattern with two more lines beginning and ending on the horizontal line. Check that no lines are too close together at any point, and that the central star is not disproportionately large or small. If something looks a little wrong or unbalanced, change it now!

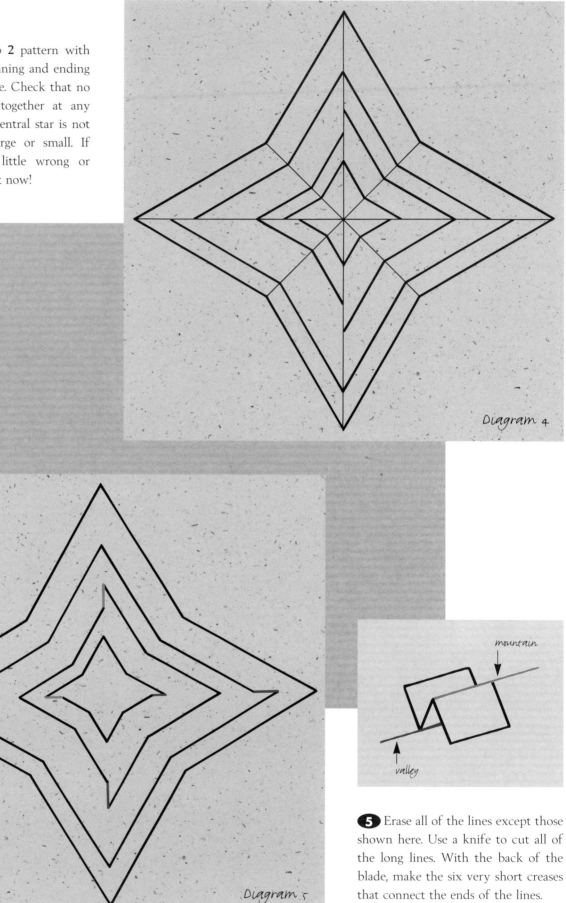

Diagram 4

Diagram 5

mountain

valley

5 Erase all of the lines except those shown here. Use a knife to cut all of the long lines. With the back of the blade, make the six very short creases that connect the ends of the lines.

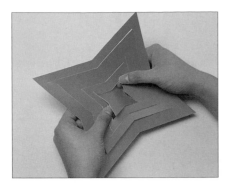

6 Hold the central star as shown. Lift the bottom point and rotate the central star through 180°.

7 When its rotation is complete, press it flat along the previously made short creases. Note that creasing is confined to two opposite points – the central part of the star remains uncreased.

RIGHT *Made from a single sheet of cardboard, the star is surprisingly 3-D. The color contrast of blue and white adds to the apparent complexity of the structure. The same twisting technique can be used in countless interesting ways. Twist concentric circles, squares, hearts, initials, or wedding bells, for example.*

Or cut different shapes for each layer of the concentric pattern, such as a banana inside an apple, inside a pear – or whatever.

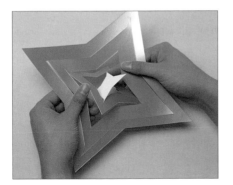

8 Repeat Step **6** with the next star, rotating the white star along with it through 180°.

9 As in Step **7**, press the star flat along two short creases. Notice how the central star becomes blue again.

10 Repeat Steps **6** and **7** with the next star. Then gently unfold each star a little, so that it pierces its neighbor at 90°. The entire design will suddenly become 3-D.

Fall leaves

Fall leaves are a perfect subject for paper sculpture: They resemble paper and their veins can be reproduced by creasing. The natural decay of leaves in the fall makes them slightly ragged, so – conveniently for us – they do not demand precision. In fact, a carefully constructed paper leaf can look unconvincing, so loosen up for this project.

Tools and Materials

knife ✪ adhesive ✪ adhesive tape ✪ foamboard ✪ cardboard

dark brown cardboard: 12x10in (30x25cm)
~ *each leaf 4⁵⁄₁₆x3½in (11x9cm)*

maroon cardboard: 12x12in (30x30cm)
~ *each leaf 5½x2¾in (14x7cm)*

mid brown cardboard: 12x10in (30x25cm)
~ *each leaf 4¾x3½in (12x9cm)*

light brown cardboard: 6x6in (15x15cm)
~ *each leaf 2¾x1⅜in (7x3.5cm)*

dark green cardboard: 10x10in (25x25cm)
~ *each leaf 4⁵⁄₁₆x2³⁄₁₆in (11x5.5cm)*

Pieces to Cut

frame 16½x12⅝in (42x32cm)
The frame's decorative waves are cut from the central panel removed from the frame
(i.e. no extra card needed)

background 16⅛x12¼in (41x31cm)

Note

Templates are 50% size

1 Roughly draw the outline of a leaf. You can use a template if you are mass-producing them. Then cut out the shape somewhat imprecisely, so that no two leaves are identical.

2 Score the leaf to create veins. Their exact location is unimportant, provided that they fan out from the stem. The position of the scores should vary from leaf to leaf, and some should be slightly curved.

3 Bend the scores, as shown, so that they alternate in a mountain/valley pattern to create a pleated effect (see *zigzag pleats*, p.19). Note the gently curved scores at the center.

ABOVE *Glue and tape the windswept pile of leaves into position before framing. Some leaves may be added later to overlap the frame. Separate the frame from the background with foamboard to increase the depth of the image. They are quick and easy to make, so family and friends could help you mass-produce them. The same leaves in shades of green could be part of a spring or summer relief scene.*

A pop-up created from a single sheet of cardboard has an elegance and ingenuity that is always admired. The play of light over the cuts and creases means that, carefully displayed, even the simplest pop-up will look dramatic. Children love making pop-ups, and the project shown here can be cut with safety scissors. For a change of look, lengthen or shorten the facial features, cut a different mouth or view from the "back."

Pop-up head

Tools and Materials

✪ knife (or scissors) ✪
pink cardboard 6x8in (15x20cm)
~*folds in half to become 3x8in (7.5x20cm)*

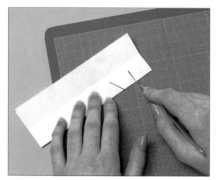

1 Fold the cardboard in half, lengthwise. Crease and unfold two quarter creases, front and back. Make two cuts through both layers at the center crease, as shown. Neatness is not critical, so cut them freehand.

2 Crease three triangles folded back from the cuts. Note that the nose crease is much longer than the mouth creases.

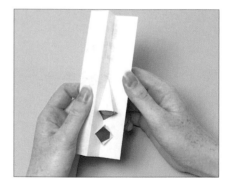

3 Unfold the three triangles. Then open the center crease and push the triangles up through it to create a pop-up nose and pair of lips (see the *pop-ups technique*, p.20).

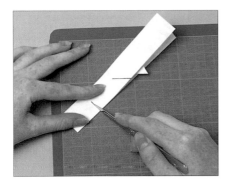

4 Refold the quarter creases made in Step **1**, so that the cardboard is now four layers thick. Make two cuts to the quarter creases, as shown, cutting through all layers.

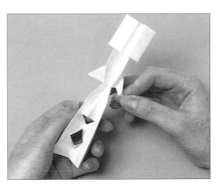

5 Crease the hair and eyes, as shown. The hair creases are parallel to the quarter creases and run off the top edge. The eye creases are at about 45° to the crease. Note the two extra creases on each eye triangle.

6 Make two rectangular pop-ups to form the hair pleat. Collapse the V creases in the eyes (see the *zigzag pleats technique*, p.19).

7 Turn the head over and tuck in the four corners.

RIGHT *Stand the head unsupported by opening the center crease below the mouth to approximately 90°. You can create a more complex hairstyle by repeating the pleating technique (Step 6) across the top on each mountain fold. As you open and close the finished pop-up, the mouth becomes animated and appears to speak. You can isolate this appealing effect and use it by itself in the center crease of a regular greeting card.*

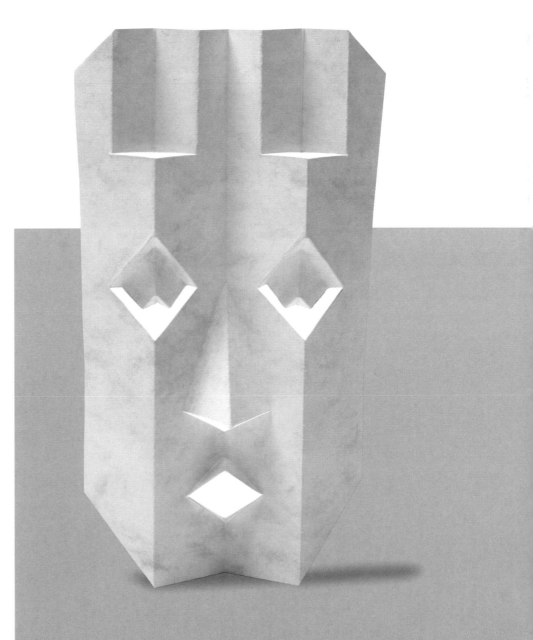

Cylinder abstract

Not everyone feels

comfortable drawing animals or objects, and lots of people enjoy creating abstract patterns. In fact, the challenges can be just as demanding – and as rewarding: colors must be chosen with care and arranged with considerable sensitivity. This project needs paper of about the same weight as this page: cardboard is too thick to roll into small cylinders.

Tools and Materials

solid dowel or other cylinder shape ✪
adhesive ✪ colored paper: red, dark pink,
light pink, blue

4 sheets paper 8x6in (20x15cm)
in each color

4 sheets paper 8x3in (20x7.5cm)
in each color

4 sheets paper 8x1½in (20x3.75cm)
in each color

(roll above rectangles to make cylinders)

yellow paper 20x24in (50x60cm)
(for background)

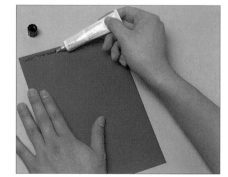

1 Take a rectangle of paper and test for the grain (see p.14): it should run along the cylinder, not around it. Apply a strip of glue along one end of the sheet, in the direction of the grain. Limit the amount of adhesive near the outer edges.

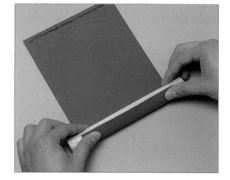

2 Working from the unglued end, begin to roll the paper around a solid cylinder, such as a length of dowel or the barrel of a thick marker pen.

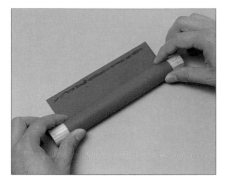

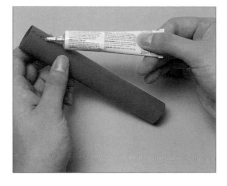

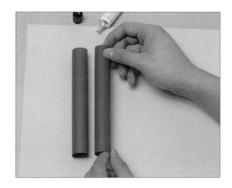

3 Continue to roll the paper, checking that the edges remain parallel. This will probably mean adjusting the roll before securing it to the strip of glue.

4 When the cylinder is fully rolled and glued, slip the dowel out. Apply a line of adhesive along the outside of the cylinder, close to the edge glued in Step **1**. Keep the line straight.

5 Lower the cylinder onto the backing sheet, adhesive side down, and glue it exactly in line with the one already in position. Take your time!

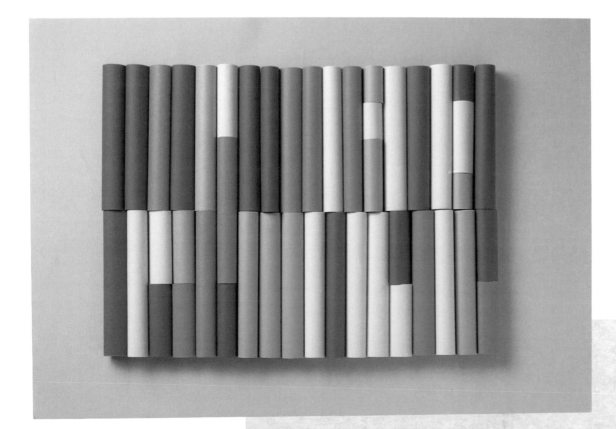

RIGHT *Though technically simple, the design can look highly effective lit from the side to create a corrugated look, and will enliven the dullest wall. More decorative cylinders can be made from paper that is pre-crumpled, slit, creased, rolled from triangles — and so on. Don't be afraid to use your imagination, because some of your experiments are sure to be a success.*

Tools and Materials

knife ✪ adhesive ✪ foamboard
✪ cardboard or paper

pink paper 8x6in (20x15cm)
cream paper 12x5in (30x12cm)
gold paper 8x6in (20x15cm)
green paper 9½x6½in (24x16cm)
blue paper 20x10in (50x25cm)
gray paper 2⅜x2⅜in(6x6cm)

Pieces to cut

cream body: 11¹³⁄₁₆x4¾in (30x12cm)
cream mouth: 2x1³⁄₁₆in (5x3cm)
(mouth can be made from body wastage)

pink fins: 7⅞x2⅜in (20x6cm),
5⅛x2⅜in (13x6cm)~*both can
be cut from one larger piece:
8x6in (20x15cm)*

pink eye: ½in (1.4cm) diameter
circle ~ *can be cut from fins wastage*

gold tail: 5¹⁵⁄₁₆x5¹⁵⁄₁₆in (15x15cm)
gold gill: 3⅛x2in (8x5cm)
gold head: 3⅛x3½in (8x9cm)
~ *all gold pieces can be cut from one
larger piece 8x6in (20x15cm)*

green reeds: 6⁵⁄₁₆x6⁵⁄₁₆in (16x16cm),
4⁵⁄₁₆x4⁵⁄₁₆in (11x11cm) ~ *both can
be cut from one larger piece
9½x6½in (24x16cm)*

blue eye: 1⅛in (2.8cm)
diameter circle

4 gray bubbles: 1⅛in (2.8cm)
diameter circles

blue background 17¼x19⅞in
(44x50cm)

*5 torn background strips: each
17¼x4in (44x10cm) (approx.)*

Fish

The subtle marbled effect of the colored cardboards enhances the appeal of this design, though it would also look good in white. Color in paper sculpture is often ornamental rather than functional: It is the play of light and shadow that informs the eye about the subject. These muted shades strike a balance between the pronounced light and dark contrasts that would be apparent on an all-white relief and the decorative impact of stronger colors.

Note
Templates are 50% size

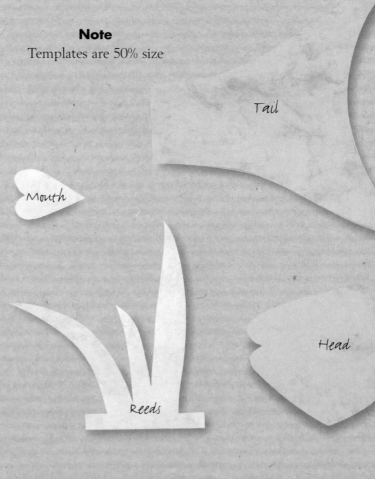

Tail

Mouth

Reeds

Head

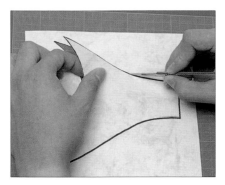

1 Cut out all the shapes. This is the tail. The template shapes and sizes for this project are just a guide, so change them as you wish.

2 Crease the tail as shown, using an upturned blade. Make sure that the crease pattern is symmetrical on each side of an imaginary line down the middle of the tail.

3 Pleat the creases as shown. The first crease on each side of the center is a valley, then the two sets of pleats continue symmetrically to the outer edges.

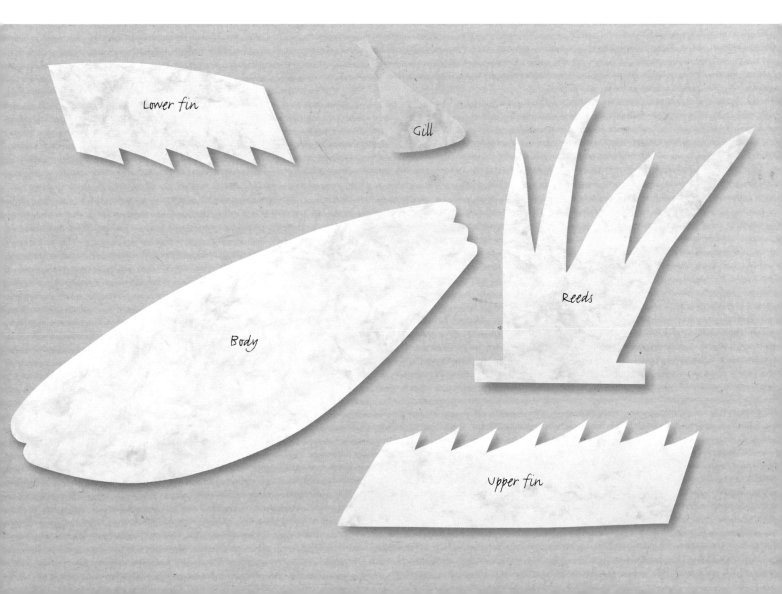

Lower fin

Gill

Reeds

Body

Upper fin

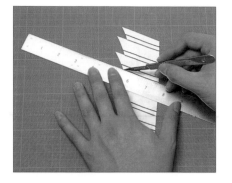

4 Cut out both sets of pink fins. Crease as indicated, so that all the creases are parallel. Note that the creases are not equally spaced, but occur in repeating pairs.

5 Collapse the creases to form a long stepped pleat. Repeat the creasing and pleating pattern on the other fin.

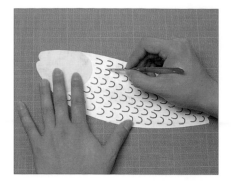

6 Glue the head to the body, checking that they align exactly. Make a series of semicircular cuts in the body. This can be done freehand, or following pencil-drawn marks on the back of the piece.

7 Lift the scales to catch the light. Try to bend them all by the same amount, or their varying angles will produce different tones.

8 Glue the tab on the gill fin and attach it below the headpiece. Bend the fin away from the body.

9 Overlap the torn strips to form the background. Align the edges into a neat rectangle, and glue the strips to one another.

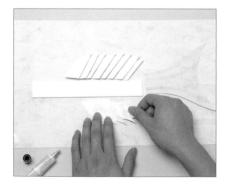

10 Paste the tail into place. Glue a strip of foamboard to the background where the body will go. Then position (but do not glue) the large body piece to indicate where the two main fins should be located. Glue the fins down.

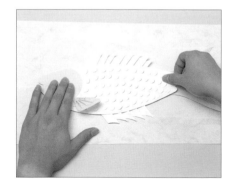

11 Apply some adhesive to the foamboard and replace the body, adjusting its position in relation to the fins and tail.

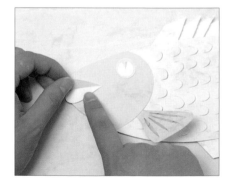

12 Glue the blue eye circle to the head, and the yellow piece on top. The yellow shape is cut from the edge to the center. Crease a triangle segment to stand upright to cast a shadow. Crease and glue down the mouth.

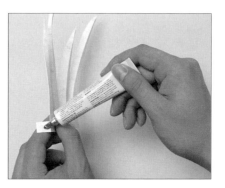

13 Crease the reed pieces to form a pleat. The creases may be made imprecisely – too much neatness can look unnatural.

14 Apply glue to the front surface of the reed tabs. Be careful not to apply it to the rear surface! It's an easy mistake to make.

15 Fold the tabs back and glue them to the bottom edge of the background, so that they overlap the fish but do not obscure any important parts.

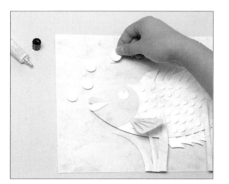

16 Glue tiny pieces of foamboard to the background to support the bubbles.

17 Dot the supports with adhesive and apply the bubbles.

BELOW *Lit from the left, the scales are very pale and the fin pleats very dark. If the light was positioned on the right, the effect would be reversed. When planning a sculpture for a particular location, keep the prevailing light conditions in mind, so as to maximize their impact. Lit from the top, for example, the fish would be barely recognizable: the important shadows would weaken, and the minor ones be too strong.*

Rooster

The *curved crease technique* (see p.17) is ideal for creating feathers, and is used extensively in this project. Construction is simple, because it is not necessary for you to position the feather pieces with complete accuracy when you assemble them. The brilliant colors of the plumage play a strong decorative role, and the plain, contrasting background keeps attention on the rooster.

Tools and Materials

knife ✪ adhesive
✪ masking tape ✪ cardboard or paper

dark blue paper 14x16in (35x41cm)
yellow paper 8x8in (20x20cm)
orange paper 5½x7½in (14x19cm)
red paper 8x10in (20x25cm)

Pieces to Cut

dark blue background
14x16in (35x41cm)
yellow pieces:
~ *all can be cut from a sheet
8x8in (20x20cm)*
head: 2¾x2¾in (7x7cm)
neck: 3¹⁵⁄₁₆x4⁵⁄₁₆in (10x11cm)
legs: 4⁵⁄₁₆x3⅛in (11x8cm)

orange piece: 5½x7½in (14x19cm)

red pieces:
~ *can be cut from a sheet
8x10in (20x25cm)*
tail: 5¹⁵⁄₁₆x6¹¹⁄₁₆in (15x17cm)
back: 3⅛x5½in (8x14cm)
comb: 1½x2¾in (4x7cm)
crop: 1½x¾in (4x2cm)

Note
Templates are 50% size

Head

Orange feathers

Tail

Comb or Cockscomb

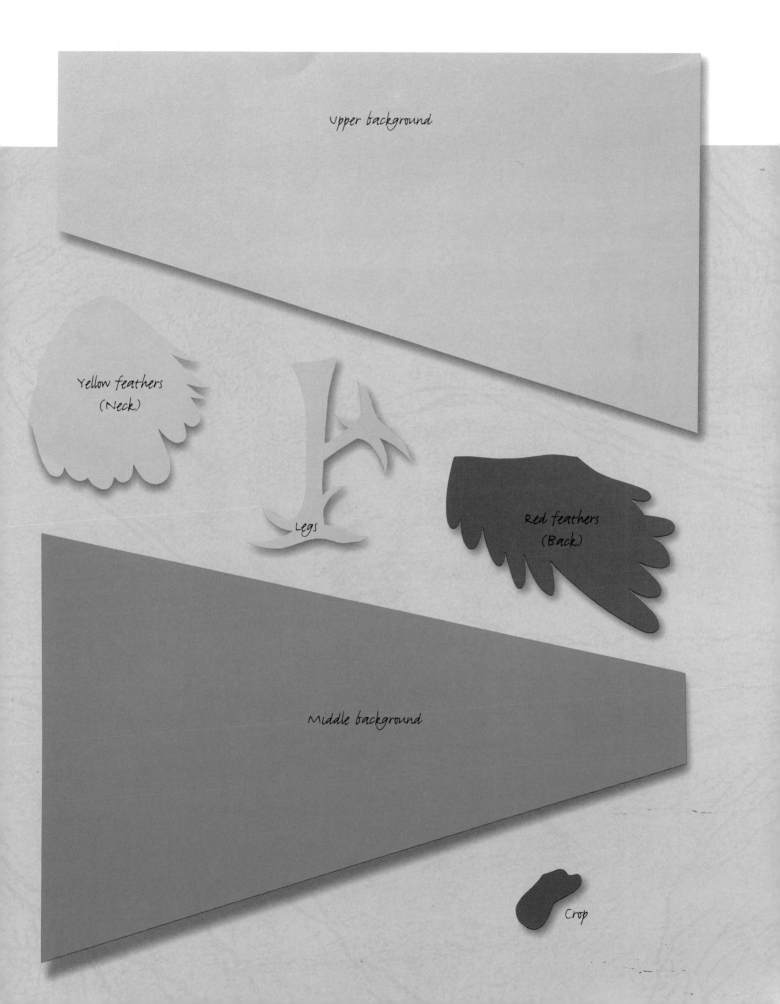

Upper background

Yellow feathers
(Neck)

Legs

Red feathers
(Back)

Middle background

Crop

1 Cut out each piece. This piece sits on the top of the back. Precision is not important here, so long as the impression of feathers is given.

2 With an upturned blade, crease all of the feather pieces. You do not need to place every score exactly, but you can use the photograph (*right*) of the finished project as a guide. Gently pleat the creases (see *pleats*, p.18).

3 Cut a pattern of small V shapes in the head piece, and a line of jagged "feathers" running from the bottom edge to a point near the eye, as shown in this view of the reverse of the head. Overlap across the cut line to create a very shallow cone (see *crimping*, p.26).

4 Secure the overlap with a small strip of masking tape. Be careful not to make the cone too pointed – it is an easy mistake to make.

5 Turn the head piece over. Gently curl the V cuts upward, with your finger. Glue the tab of the comb piece behind the top of the head. Note the curved creases on the comb.

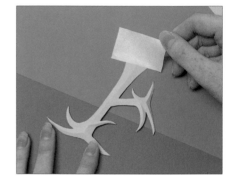

6 Score the leg piece as shown. Tape it to the assembled background. The technique is similar to that of scoring in the *Nameplate* project (p.46).

7 The feather pieces can now go into place. Begin with the tail, judging its position in relation to the feet.

8 Add the orange feather units, taping each layer in turn.

9 Attach the red body feathers in the same way.

10 Glue the head and neck to the background, and add the red crop piece beneath the beak.

ABOVE *The Rooster is an example of the classical style of relief paper sculpture, owing more to drawing and collage than to engineering or constructional skills. You can use the same layering technique to make other birds, or omit the pleating to create the fur of cats or shaggy dogs. The only tricky part is designing the head, but if you do this last, you will find it much easier.*

Valentine mobile

An ingenious twisting technique permits the arrow to pierce the heart, in this effective 3-D mobile. The secret lies in two tiny creases across the middle of the arrow which must be placed precisely, so practice first on a spare piece of cardboard. This technique can be used to achieve more complex 3-D forms, such as the *Twist-out star* (p.68).

Tools and Materials

knife ✪ thread ✪ hole punch
(or needle)
red cardboard 10x8in (25x20cm)
(backed with a different color)

1 Draw and cut out a heart which is sufficiently wide to accommodate a long arrow.

Note
Template is 50% size

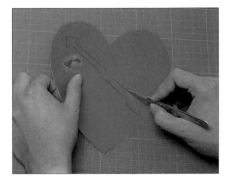

2 Draw the arrow diagonally across the heart. Note the "step" in the middle of the arrow making the halves appear misaligned. Cut around each half of the arrow, but not across the "step", as this is the connecting section.

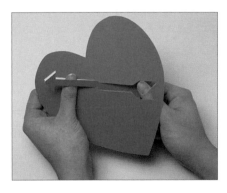

3 Hold the heart and bend the tip of the arrow forward and the feathers backward as shown.

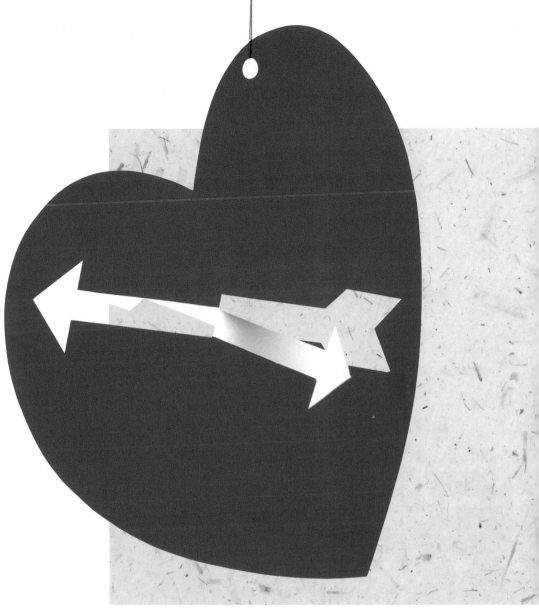

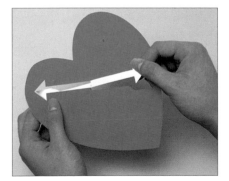

4 Continue until you have turned the arrow through 180° so that it points backwards. Create two tiny creases at the "step" by pressing the cardboard flat. Unfold the arrow a little, so that it pierces the heart at 90°.

5 Make a hole with a punch or a needle for the thread to pass through.

ABOVE *Instead of using light and shade (as most paper sculpture does), the mobile exploits negative and positive forms and the two faces of the cardboard to create a strikingly 3-D effect. The technique provides an excellent alternative to a conventional greeting card: it can be mailed flat but becomes 3-D when the planes of arrow and heart are separated. Adapt the "step" method to other shapes inside the heart, such as initials or flowers.*

Steam train

Although this is one of the more complex projects in the book, the steam train is easier to make than it looks, because most of the pieces are geometric and so, easy to draw and cut out. The colors can be changed, or you can use all white – the result will still be spectacular. You should pay particular attention to the foamboard supports that raise parts of the train at varying levels above the background. They must be sturdy, but not so bulky that they are visible, and be placed at the correct height in relation to one another.

Tools and Materials & Pieces to Cut

tracing paper ✪ knife
✪ adhesive ✪ foamboard ✪
masking tape ✪ cardboard

background: *Overall dimensions 16½x9½in (42x24cm)*
blue mountains: 16½x5⅛in (42x13cm)
green hills: 16½x4¾in (42x12cm)
tracing paper: 16½x11¹³⁄₁₆in (42x30cm)
train: dark green ~ *all pieces can be cut from a sheet 7¹⁄₁₆x10¼in (18x26cm)*
individual pieces:
chassis: 9¹³⁄₁₆x2in (25x5cm)
boiler: 3¹⁵⁄₁₆x6¹¹⁄₁₆in (10x17cm)
aft funnel piece: 2¹⁄₁₆x⅜in (5.2x1cm)
red ~ *all pieces can be cut from a sheet 7⅞x4¾in (20x12cm)*

individual pieces:
cab: 3½x3½in (9x9cm)
2 large wheels: 1½in (4cm) diameter
2 small wheels: ¾in (2cm) diameter
snow plough: 1⅜x1¹⁄₁₆in (3.5x2.7cm)
fore funnel: 1¾x1¾in (4.5x4.5cm)

yellow ~ *all pieces can be cut from a sheet 3½x1¾in (9x4.5cm)*
individual pieces:

aft funnel: 2¼x¾in (5.7x2cm)
drive shaft housing: ¹⁵⁄₁₆x¾in (2.3x2cm)
4 boiler stripes, each 3½x⅛in (9cmx3mm)
3 fore funnel stripes: 1½x⅜in (4x1cm) and 2 at 1½x³⁄₁₆in (4cmx5mm)
light gray: smoke: 11¹³⁄₁₆x5½in (30x14cm)
2 large wheel rims, each 1¾in (4.5cm) diameter
2 small wheel rims, each ¹⁵⁄₁₆in (2.3cm) diameter

dark gray: 2 drive shafts
fore shaft: 3⁵⁄₁₆x³⁄₁₆in (8.5cmx5mm)
aft shaft: 3¾x³⁄₁₆in (9.5cmx5mm)

6 tiny circles:
2 white *(on drive shafts)*, each ⅛in (4mm) in diameter
2 black *(at center of large wheels)*, each ³⁄₁₆in (5mm) diameter
2 black *(at center of small wheels)*, each ⅛in (3mm) diameter

foreground:
dark gray cinders: 13x⅜in (33x1cm)
dark brown sleepers: 13x⅜in (33x1cm)
beige foreground: 13³⁄₁₆x1½in (33.5x3.7cm)

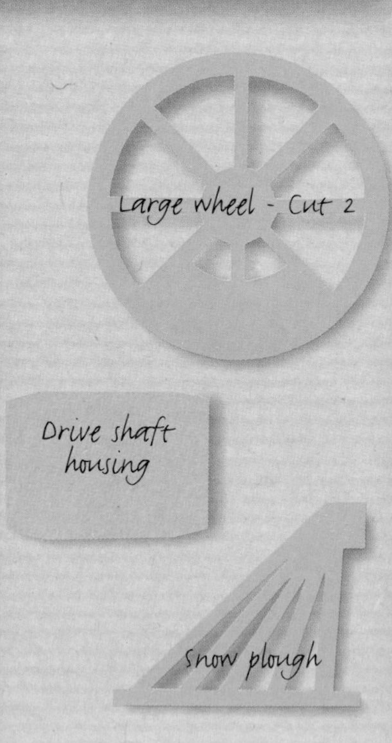

Large wheel - Cut 2

Drive shaft housing

snow plough

Cab

Fore drive shaft

Note
Use this template for the aft drive shaft, but add ⅜in (1cm) to the top

Large wheel rim - Cut 2

Note Use the wheel and wheel rim template at 50% for the small wheels

Funnel

Funnel decoration

Funnel

Background A

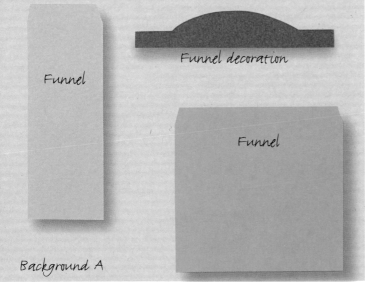

Pieces to Cut

trimmings:

yellow rectangle 3½x⅛in (9cmx3mm) ~ *cut 4*

yellow rectangle 2½x⅜in (4x1cm) ~ *cut 3*

yellow rectangle 1½x³⁄₁₆in (4cmx5mm) ~ *cut 2*

gray circle wheel rim 1¾in (4.5cm) diameter ~ *cut 2*

gray circle wheel rim ¹⁵⁄₁₆in (2.3cm) diameter ~ *cut 2*

dark gray rectangle 3⁵⁄₁₆x³⁄₁₆in (8.5cmx5mm)

red square 9¹³⁄₁₆x9¹³⁄₁₆in (25x25cm)

gray circle wheel rim ¹⁵⁄₁₆in (2.3cm) diameter ~ *cut 2*

gray circle wheel rim ¹⁵⁄₁₆in (2.3cm) diameter ~ *cut 2*

Note
Templates on background A are 100% size and the templates on background B are 50% size

Boiler

Background B

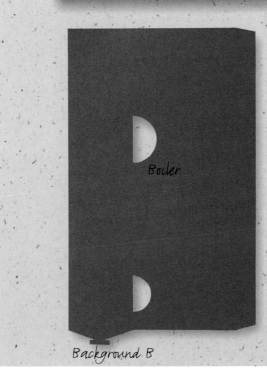

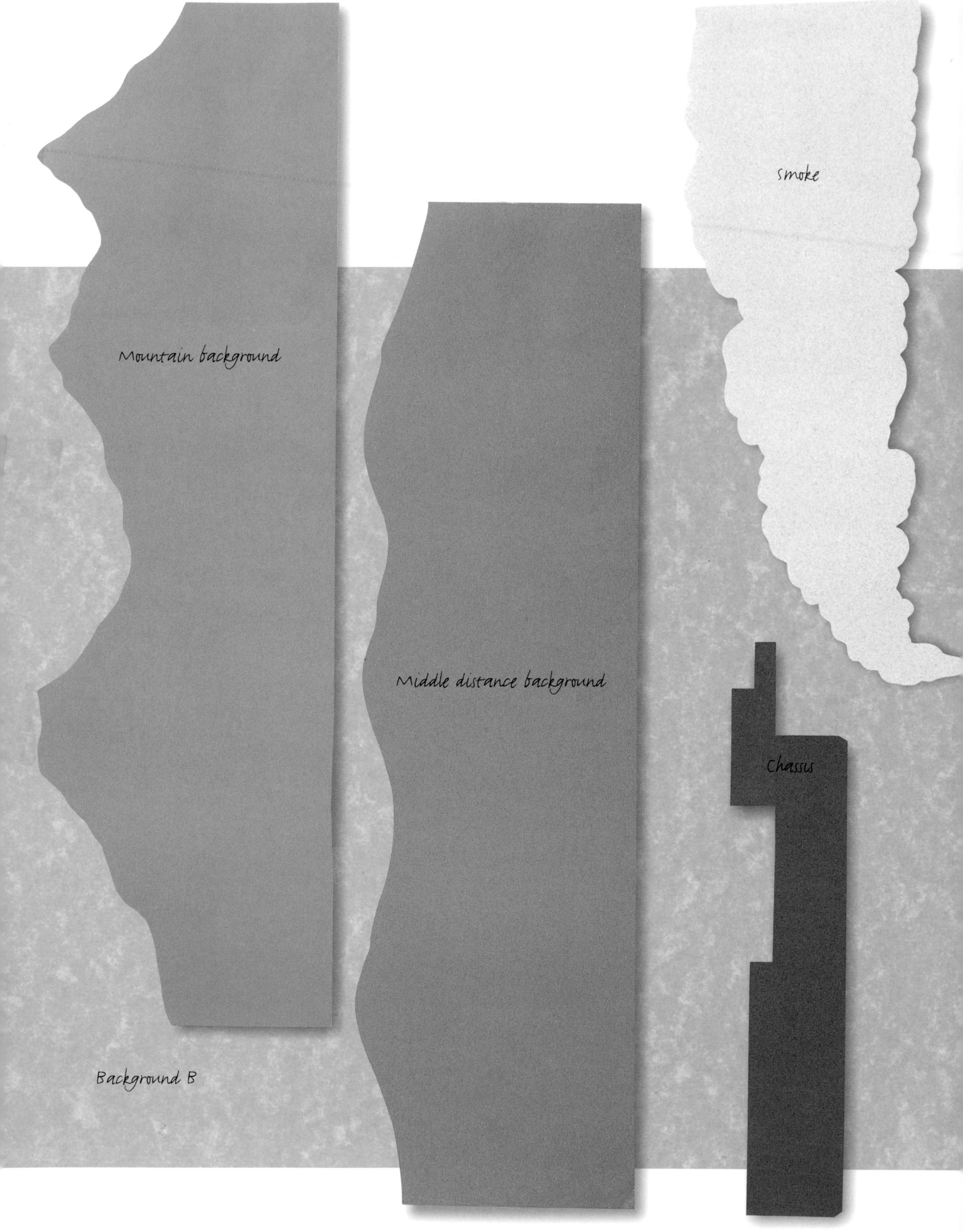

Mountain background

Middle distance background

smoke

Chassis

Background B

sleepers

Foreground

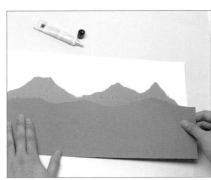

1 Glue the colored landscape pieces to the backing sheet. The mountains should be jagged for visual interest.

2 Cover the entire background with tracing paper. This softens the colors, helping the train to stand out.

3 Fold the tracing paper over the back of the sheet and fasten it with masking tape.

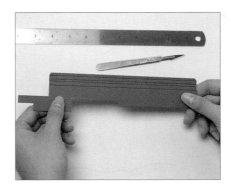

4 This is the chassis piece. Draw four parallel creases on it, as shown.

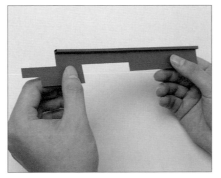

5 Make the creases with an upturned blade, creating a thin, open box along the top edge of the chassis. Glue the top edge of the cardboard to the front of the chassis to complete the box.

6 This is the boiler piece with the two crease marks drawn on it.

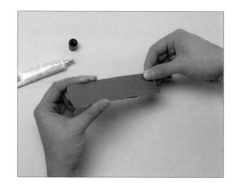

7 Crease the boiler and then bend it into a semicircle. This will be easier if the grain of the cardboard runs along the length of the boiler (see *grain*, p.14).

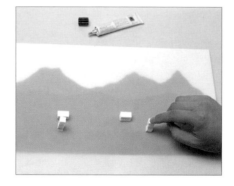

8 Glue the tab in place to complete the boiler.

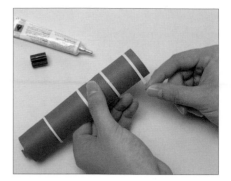

9 Add four narrow yellow strips to the boiler, gluing the ends of the strips to the flat face which will be the back.

10 Insert and glue the two funnels into the holes in the top of the boiler. Make sure they are exactly vertical. The funnels are made in exactly the same way as the boiler.

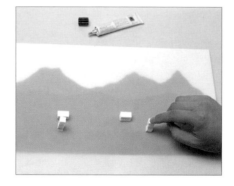

11 Glue two sets of foamboard supports to the background. The top pair are two layers high; the lower ones four layers high. They must be well hidden from view.

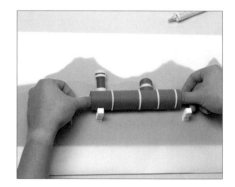

12 Glue the boiler to the upper foamboard supports, making sure that it is exactly horizontal. This is the single most important alignment on the sculpture, so be precise.

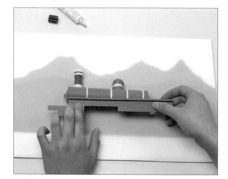

13 Glue the chassis to the higher supports, so that it covers the bottom edge of the boiler. Check that it is horizontal against the background, and parallel to the top of the boiler.

14 This is the train's cab. Make four horizontal and one vertical crease in it, as shown.

15 Form the creases, gluing the top of the cab to create a box section similar to that on the chassis.

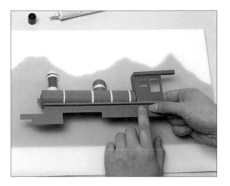

16 Glue the bottom edge of the cab behind the top edge of the chassis so that the front face of the cab fits snugly against the back of the boiler.

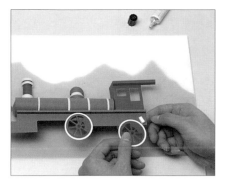

17 Assemble and glue the wheels. Attach two small foamboard supports to the chassis, one for each wheel, and glue the wheels into position.

18 Bend the yellow drive shaft housing into a semicircle and glue it to the chassis by means of a tab at each end.

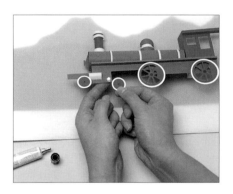

19 Complete the front wheels and attach them to the tops of two tiny foamboard supports which are already glued to the chassis. Check that the bottoms of the four wheels are aligned to each other.

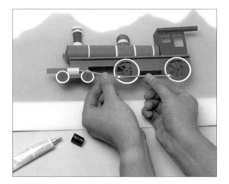

20 Join the two sections of drive shaft rod, adding a white disk at the joint, and another at the back end. Check that the front end fits into the housing, and that the joint and back end touch the rims of the big wheels before gluing.

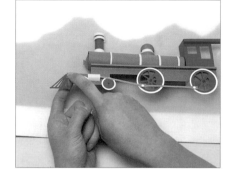

21 Glue the snow plough (also known as a "cow pusher") to the front, as shown. The bottom of the plough should be aligned to the bottom of the wheels.

22 Curl the edge of the smoke shape by pulling the cardboard between your thumb and a knife handle. Notice the cuts, which add important details to this large piece.

23 Stiffen the smoke shape by gluing two long foamboard strips to it. Add layers of foamboard to the strips to raise the smoke to the level of the funnel.

24 Glue the foamboard supports to the background, carefully inserting the smoke into the funnel.

25 Attach the brown sleeper to the gray cinders. This is a little tricky because the rail is a delicate shape, so do it with care.

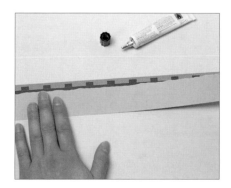

26 Glue the beige foreground over the bottom edge of the rail. Check that the long, thin foreground pieces are accurately aligned.

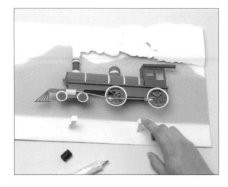

27 Build two foamboard supports beneath the train, one thickness of foamboard higher than the chassis supports.

28 Glue the pale foreground section to the foamboard supports, aligning the top edge with an imaginary line just above the bottoms of the wheels.

BELOW *The techniques used here to construct half cylinders, box sections, and wheels, all lifted from the background on foamboard supports, can be adapted to many kinds of trains and other vehicles. Vintage cars are especially suitable, because they are "boxier" than modern streamlined automobiles. All you need to begin is a good side view of the vehicle, and a three-quarter image to show relative depths and layerings.*

Cloudscape

When does a flat paper collage become a relief sculpture? There can be no precise answer, except perhaps that the sculpture uses light and shadow to separate the layers whereas a collage relies on color. Notice the importance of the shadows under the cloud and the light catching the tops of the hills in this relief.

Tools and Materials

knife ✪ adhesive ✪
3 sheets of white cardboard each
15¾x11¾in (40x30cm)
~ 2 frame pieces: Each 15¾x11¾in (40x30cm)
~ clouds and landscape pieces: Torn from one
large sheet 15¾x11¾in (40x30cm)
Colored paper:
sky: Cream paper 15¾x11¾in (40x30cm)
sun: Yellow paper 1½x1½in (4x4cm)
sea: Blue paper (3 different shades)
each 6x2in (15x5cm)

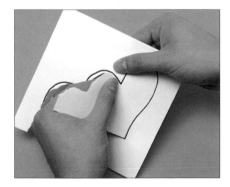

1 Draw a full-sized pencil sketch of the entire image and amend it until it looks good. Draw the shapes onto cardboard and tear them out. You may need to tear the same shape out a few times to get it right, because tearing is much less precise than cutting, but tearing too cautiously can also spoil the effect.

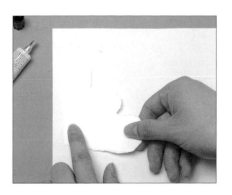

2 Glue the shapes to the background. It is wise to cut and tear all the shapes before beginning to glue, so that any necessary adjustments can be made.

ABOVE *Tearing is fun and an expressive technique, but it needs some care if the results are not to look sloppy. Note how the cut and colored sun and the sea create a strong contrast to the torn white shapes. The two layers of torn frame play an important role in the project: without them, the composition would look too "loose."*

The dove makes effective use of the *inside crimp technique* (p.26). It is based on an origami dove which was folded

Dove

from an uncut square – as all true origami must be. The only slight modification was to cut the wing and tail feathers to give a more expressive outline. Many origami creatures can be adapted into paper sculpture by shaping the edges of the sheet. Purists may protest, but the results can be very impressive.

Tools and Materials

knife ✪ ruler (or straight edge) ✪ black fiber-tip pen ✪ thread ✪ needle (or hole punch) ✪ white stiff paper 11¾x16in (30x40cm) ~ *folds in half to become 11¾x8in (30x20cm).*

❶ Fold the paper in half. Try to fold either straight along the grain (see p.14) or perpendicularly across it. This will help the bird hang symmetrically, because the tensions in the paper will be symmetrical.

❷ With the help of a straight edge and the back of a pointed blade, make two creases through both layers of cardboard in the positions shown.

When unfolded your cut out shape should look like this.

Note
Template is 50% size.

3 Collapse the creases as shown, so that the two holes through which the thread will pass are turned inward toward the wings (see the *inside crimp*, p.26).

ABOVE *The dove is a graceful sculpture which looks best among others. To maximize rotation, place the birds in moving air: in a hallway, near a window, above a radiator, or over a bed. The design folds flat and can be mailed as a gift.*

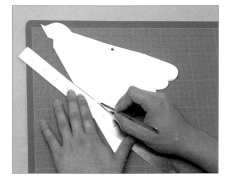

4 Unfold the Step **3** creases. Make a further crease between the center crease and the sharp angle that separates the wing from the tail.

5 Push the tail up between the two wings, along the Step **4** creases.

6 Unfold the Step **5** creases. Make a short crease across the neck (for the clearest view of its position, see the photograph of the finished dove).

7 Form the creases, turning the head inside out, so that the inside surface of the paper is brought into view.

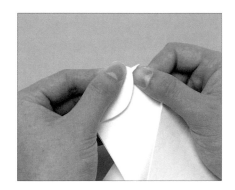

8 Make two minute creases for the beak. These are identical to the creases in Step **3**, but much smaller. They are too tiny to indent with an upturned blade, so make them by hand.

9 Refold all the creases to create the finished dove. To suspend it, pass thread through the holes. Draw the eyes with a black fiber-tip pen.

Fun monster puppet

Here is a project to play with. You can insert your fingers at the back of the jaws to make them "snap!" Children will love it. This simple mechanism brings the puppet into the realms of paper engineering, but the construction techniques are similar to those used elsewhere in this book. You can make an entire collection of monster heads in this way, perhaps attaching them to "bodies" that would hang in front of your forearm. The fun thing about designing a monster is that no one knows what such creatures look like, so you can make whatever curiosity you want – in whatever way you find easiest!

Tools and Materials

knife ✪ adhesive ✪ masking tape ✪ pair of compasses ✪ paper fasteners ✪ straight edge (or ruler) ✪ hole punch ✪ cardboard

Pieces to Cut

green cardboard 17¾x21¾in (45x55cm)
~ individual pieces:
jaws 9¹⁄₁₆x16½in (23x42cm) – cut 2,
nostrils 3⅛x2³⁄₁₆in (8x5.5cm),
eye support 9¹³⁄₁₆x2¾in (25x7cm)

white cardboard 10½x8in (27x20cm)
~ individual pieces:
lower teeth 7⅞x2¾in (20x7cm) ~ cut 2,
upper teeth 6⁵⁄₁₆x2⅜in (16x6cm) ~ cut 2

orange cardboard *(ears)* 9¾x17¾in (25x45cm)

red cardboard *(tongue)* 12½x4¼in (32x11cm)

yellow cardboard *(eyes)* 10¼x5⅛in (26x13cm)~ *cut 2, each 5⅛in (13cm) diameter*

blue cardboard *(eyebrows)* 6¼x3½in (16x9cm) ~ *cut 2, each 6⁵⁄₁₆x1½in 16x4cm*

*Upper teeth
(cut one, flip and cut another so that you get symmetrical pieces to make a pair)*

*Lower teeth
(cut one, flip and cut another so that you get symmetrical pieces to make a pair)*

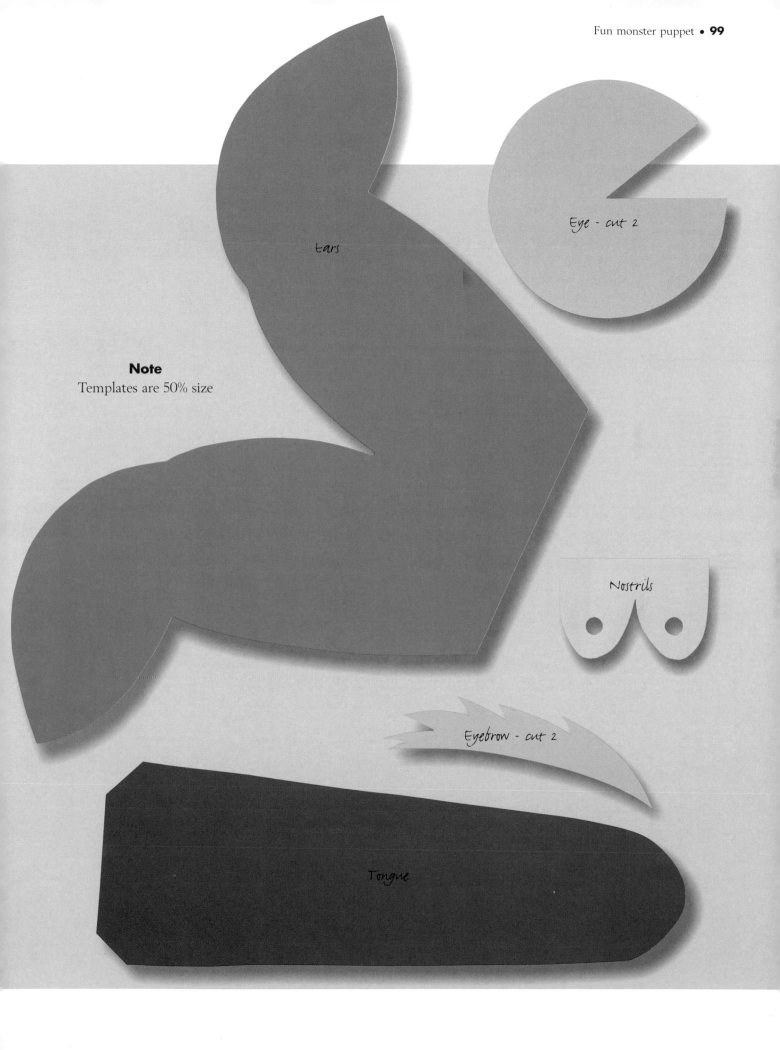

Ears

Eye - cut 2

Note
Templates are 50% size

Nostrils

Eyebrow - cut 2

Tongue

Jaw - cut 2

Eye support

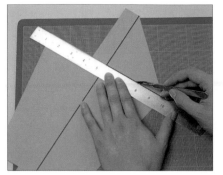

1 With an upturned blade and a straight edge, make the creases on both the jaw pieces.

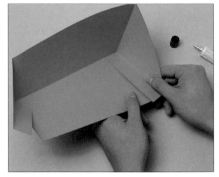

2 Carefully fold up and glue each of the jaw halves.

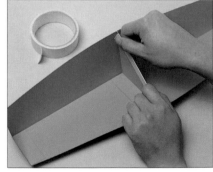

3 Join the *larger* ends of the pieces with masking tape. Make sure that the tape goes on smoothly.

4 Apply another strip of tape to the outside of the joint. This should make a strong hinge between the jaws, capable of withstanding the most ferocious "snapping."

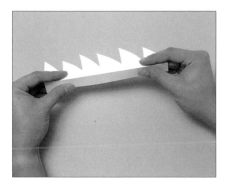

5 Crease a tab along each of the four rows of teeth.

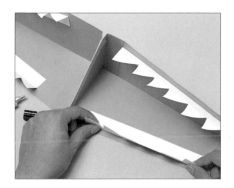

6 Open the jaw and glue all of the teeth inside. Note that the two shorter rows go at the front of the upper jaw.

7 Crease a tab across the base of the tongue.

8 Glue the tab and fix the tongue into the back of the lower jaw behind the larger rows of teeth.

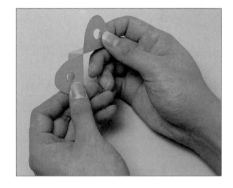

9 Crease the nostril piece as shown.

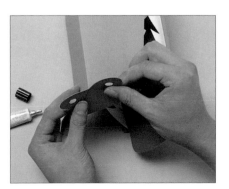

10 Glue the nostrils to the front of the upper jaw, level with the edge.

11 This is the support for the eyes. Crease it along the black lines. Note the long cuts up the middle.

12 Fold up the left and right halves, gluing the ends of each half together, as shown, to create two triangular sections. See Step **16** for clearer view.

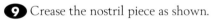

13 Cut out two circles for eyes. With a compass, draw two concentric circles, then crease them with an upturned blade.

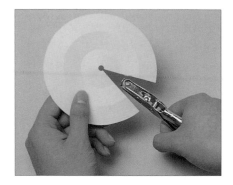

14 Punch a hole in the center of the circle, which should be at the point of the cut out section.

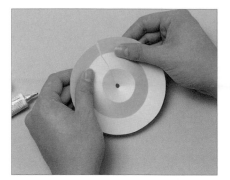

15 Bend the circle, closing the cut section, so that the creases form a concentric pleat. Carefully glue the two edges of the cut section together.

16 Pierce a hole through each eye support with a sharp pointed blade.

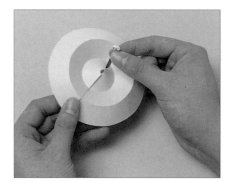

17 Push a paper fastener through the center of each eye.

18 Then put it through the hole in the eye support. Open the "wings" of the fastener to hold the eye firmly in place.

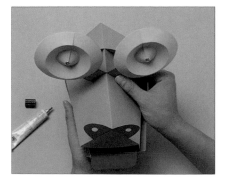

19 Repeat with the other eye, and glue the entire eye unit to the top edge of the jaw, about two-thirds of the way toward the back.

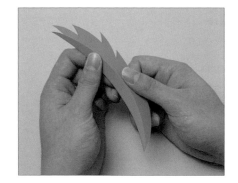

20 Crease each eyebrow piece, as shown.

21 Glue an eyebrow to the top of each eye. For neatness, make it hide the edge of the joint that runs to the center of the eye.

 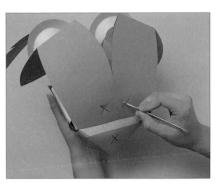 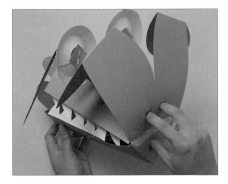

22 Fold the ears, as shown.

23 Glue the ear piece firmly to the back of the upper jaw.

24 Cut three Xs into the back of the jaws, two in the upper jaw and one in the lower. These are for your fingers, and best made smaller than you think you need – they are easier to enlarge than to reduce.

25 Push two fingers through the top Xs, and the thumb through the lower one. The cardboard should grip your fingers tightly and enable them to open and close the jaws.

RIGHT *This puppet is just one suggestion for a project that can be infinitely varied. It is easy and fun to change the proportions of the jaws, the size of the nostrils, the shape of the teeth, the length of the tongue, the position of the eyes, and the appearance of the ears, to make any number of monster relatives. Use white cardboard and paint it for another original touch.*

GALLERY

There are three steps to learning a new art or craft: learning the techniques; gaining experience using them; and using them expressively by following the orthodox techniques when they are appropriate — or ignoring them and devising your own. The Gallery section shows a diversity of imaginative paper sculptures ranging from traditional to radical, which should help you find your own expressive voice.

Matisse's Model

6¹/₂x9in (17x23cm)

Ron King

The artist cut through an existing book with a jig saw to create a negative image based on a Matisse figure. Recycling a book this way explores and expands the concept of what a book is, adding interest to the piece. If the work had been made from unused material, it would have lost much of its visual and intellectual subtlety.

April Showers

8x8in (20x20cm)

Kathryn Jackson

This artist comes from the English city of Manchester (reknowned for supposedly being a very rainy city), and that was the inspiration for this piece, commissioned for a book of birthday images from 365 artists. The figures are glued flat to the background, but the umbrellas are folded and stand out on wires. The artist deliberately created a repeat pattern by flattening the perspective and by crowding the image.

Pisa Boat Race

8x8in (20x20cm)

Kathryn Jackson

Market Square

8x8in (20x20cm)

Kathryn Jackson

These two works are part of a series created for an exhibition of the artist's travels in Italy. Both are made almost entirely of Italian banknotes, some of which are unrecognizable at first glance. The apparent spontaneity of the construction and the expressive use of exaggerated perspective are carefully balanced by the order imposed by wide, square frames (not shown here).

Ice Skaters: Central Park, New York

8x8in (20x20cm)

Kathryn Jackson

An unexpectedly joyous scene in a crowded urban setting inspired this piece. Note how the buildings do not stand impassively, but sway to and fro, to heighten the impression of movement in the composition, and therefore in the subject matter. The use of crumpled paper to render the trees is a surprising but appropriate technique.

Lampshades

height 18in (45cm)

Jean Mould Hart

Paper has long been used to diffuse light from a natural or artificial source, as screens and shades. Paper and light seem to have been made for each other when light falls onto a relief paper sculpture, and when light shines *through* it. In these simple lampshades – made by rolling paper into a cone – surface interest is created by texturing and embossing.

Goldfish Under Lilies

16x22in (40x55cm)

Joan Kritchman-Knuteson

In this delicate piece, the artist aimed to show several depths, using the *layering* and *blocking* techniques (see pp. 24 and 25). Notice how the lilies are mounted farther away from the background than the goldfish, so that their shadows can play an important part in the composition. Subtle color blends were achieved by layering tissue papers.

Courting Cranes

27¹/₂x16in (70x40cm)

Joan Kritchman-Knuteson

Japanese cranes symbolize faithfulness, and were chosen as an appropriate subject for this piece, made as a wedding gift. Oriental decorative papers add texture, and contrast well with the solid colors. Notice how the black sky and narrow border thrust the quiet colors forward.

Eagle

18x24in (45x60cm)

Joan Kritchman-Knuteson

Stock report pages from a newspaper, photocopied onto medium-weight paper and cut to shape, form this sculpture. The careful use of coloring, and of shadows between the layerings, along with the position of the print columns, help a quick recognition of the subject.

"Fall Vintage"

18x20in (45x50cm)

Joan Kritchman-Knuteson

Commissioned to promote Californian wineries, this piece skillfully combines paper, wood (for the lattice), and acrylic paint to achieve a rich palette of fall colors. The way in which the leaves occasionally break the frame creates additional visual interest, as does the contrast between the busy paper shapes and the quiet cream background.

Knight

37¹/₂x24x2³/₄in (95x60x7cm)

Bill Finewood

The pale colors and the delicate bending and scoring on the knight and his charger contrast effectively with the crumpled texture of the dark trees and foliage. Skillful positioning of the light source gives the armor some bright highlights that contribute to its metallic look.

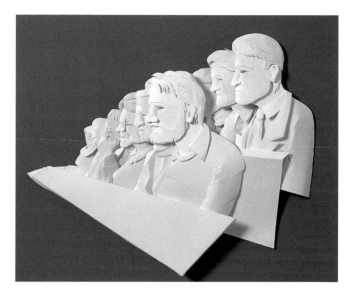

Jury

13³/₄x12in (35x30cm)

Penny Read

Judge

8¹/₂x12in (22x30cm)

Penny Read

These two pieces were made by a design student as part of a series entitled "Guilty or Not Guilty?" and are the culmination of much on-the-spot drawing and photography. Attention is deliberately focused on the judge's bright red robes, which are his symbol of power. The jurors are observed individually to demonstrate a cross-section of race, age, and class. The bold use of perspective in both pieces adds to the authenticity of the observation.

Chicken and Typewriter

Chicken 24x24x24in (60x60x60cm) approx.

Typewriter 24x24x15¹/₂in (60x60x39cm) approx.

Luned Rhys Parri

Made by gluing paper to a cardboard framework, then painting the surface, these expressive sculptures use some of the conventional techniques described in this book, but achieve a very different aesthetic. When exhibited separately, the sculptures are accompanied by chicken or typewriter noises, to help evoke the artist's childhood memories.

Cuthbert the Cat

16x16¹/₂x4in
(40x42x10cm)
Emilyn Hill
The personality, texture, and color of the artist's cat were the inspiration for this expressive sculpture. It was constructed from thick watercolor paper coated with PVA glue and sand, some of which was tinted. Note the complexity of the head contrasted against the simplicity of the body and the boldness of the abstract forms that surround the figure.

Lizard

10in (25cm) height

Pat Phillips

Here, the artist sets herself a challenge: to create a 3-D sculpture from one sheet of 17x24in (42x60cm) medium-weight paper, and to use only a sharp blade – that is, no glue or tape. The background was made in a similar way to the *Fall leaves* (p.72), enabling light and shade to play an important part in the piece. Everything locks together with *integral tabs* (p.22).

Anteater

39¹/₂in (100cm) length

Pat Phillips

This impressive creature was an experiment by the artist to see if paper and cardboard could build a large automaton with an acceptable amount of movement. It was constructed from rings of brown cardboard held together underneath with paper fasteners and along the top with loose strips of fabric that enable the body to flex until the tape is pulled taut.

Bowl

19¹/₄x4¹/₂in (49x11cm)

Lois Walpole

The form and the surface pattern of this striking bowl were achieved by interlocking preprinted postcards. The postcards were glued together in a precise design, determined after much experimentation. The bowl is surprisingly strong in the center, but weaker around the rim, though it is not intended to be used.

Waste Paper Basket

12¹/₂x29¹/₂in (32x75cm)

Lois Walpole

This waste basket – appropriately composed of wastepaper! – uses tightly rolled pages taken from a Michelin Road Atlas and a Yellow Pages telephone directory. The form effectively mimics baskets made of cane and other traditional materials, and is likewise very strong.

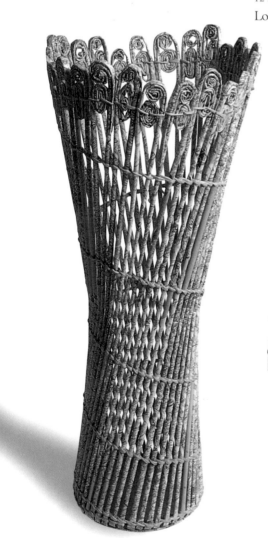

Semicircular Interior Fan

48in (120cm) span

Juliet Walker

A simple *pleating technique* (p.18) was the basis of this sophisticated and beautiful object. The paper is handmade, stiffened with wire supports and a wooden base. The surface decoration is derived from studies of coral and rock formations.

Paper Flowers

8x18in (20x45cm)

Peter Niczewski

"Necessity is the mother of invention," says the proverb. Needing a bunch of flowers, but finding the florist's store closed, the artist made his own! He learned the techniques from his father, who brought his skills to Britain from Poland and created paper sculptures for exhibitions and store window displays in the 1950s and 1960s, in common with a number of Polish emigrants at that time.

100 Year Anniversary

16x16in (40x40cm) approx.

Johnna Bandle

Intricate layerings and subtle curves combine here to wonderful effect. Notice how the numerals and decorative forms balance – neither dominates the other. Skillful positioning of the light source makes the shadows cast by the numerals very distinct, thereby aiding recognition.

"Wibberjawed"

48x48x12in (120x120x30cm)

Carol Jeanotilla

"Wibberjawed" is an old Nebraskan pioneer term for something which moves in all directions at once, and refers to the many delicately counterbalanced layers at the front of the work which vibrate when people approach or pass by! It is made mostly from heavy rag paper which has been curled, scored, crumpled, and embossed. Inspiration for the piece came from an upholstery fabric.

Dub and Talk

18x18x4in (45x45x10cm)

David Cox

This boxed piece was inspired by the Dub poetry of Jamaican deejay music. The main frame was constructed of corrugated cardboard and the sculptures were made from scrap paper and found objects glued together and sometimes painted. Although created in a sophisticated way, it retains the immediacy of folk art.

Bugs

12¹/₂x25¹/₂x3in (32x65x8cm)

David Cox

This mask was made to be held in front of the face during the telling of a story about insects. Corrugated cardboard was crushed to form the main structure., onto which colored scrap paper was glued, some of which was painted.

The Night Communicator

12x39¹/₂x3in (30x100x8cm)

David Cox

Like its companion piece *Bugs* (above), *The Night Communicator* is a mask, this time made to accompany a story about a nightmare journey. It was constructed in the same way.

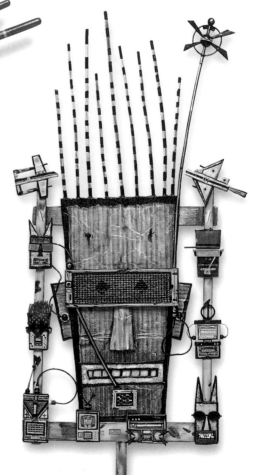

Rhino
Robert Janecek
Bull
Steve Cox
each approx. 8x12in (20x30cm)

The impact of these expressive animals is heightened by the unusual angles from which they are depicted. The brightly colored backgrounds help to define the silhouettes of the animals more clearly than white would have done.

Einstein

14x22in (35x75cm) approx.

Johnna Bandle

Paper sculpture portraits are never easy, but this one was realized with immense confidence. The aim in portraiture is not only to cut the paper into a good likeness, but also to use highlights and shadows as if they were drawn with white and black chalks. The contrast between the wild, shredded hair and the accurate layerings of the face effectively characterizes the subject as eccentric but intelligent.

3-D Swan

12x8x4in (30x20x10cm)

Relief Swan

Lifesize

David Cook

It is interesting to compare these two sculptures of the same subject by the same designer, a noted wildlife artist. Delicate curves made with the *crimping technique* (p.26) are common to both, and effectively capture the sweeping form of the wings. The large curved planes and the detailed feathered edge on the wings form a contrast – and help to draw the viewer's eye into the sculptures. Note also the importance of the light to both sculptures, particularly the relief. The absence of color on the two heads, devoid of gratuitous decoration, creates a feeling of dignity.

Braided Paper Shopping Bags

Both lifesize

Mary Butcher

These related bags are made from strips of folded newspaper, braided together. They were inspired by reading that in northwest England in the 1890s, newspapers were recycled into bags for carrying fish. The technique survives in the Philippines, where old newspapers are braided to make boxes, bags, and folders.

Standing Abstract

12in high (30cm)

Bill Blanco

Paper is a versatile material and it is not obvious at first sight that this sculpture was made from cardboard. It could equally well have been constructed from painted wood, papier mâché, or metal. Separate pieces of cardboard were cut for each face and then tabbed together.

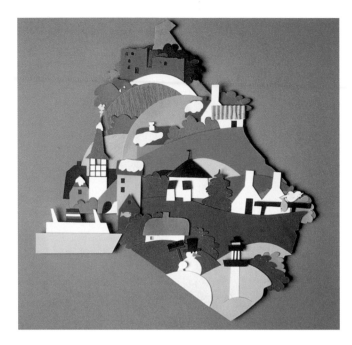

The Island of Bornholm

12x12in (30x30cm)

Soren Thaae

The unusual shape of this *layered relief* has great impact, and the skillful use of many colors encourages the eye to explore the detail. It was commissioned as the cover for a ferry timetable – hence the inclusion of a ferry in the bottom corner.

The Balcony

2¹/₂x5¹/₂x³/₈in (6.5x14x1cm)

Soren Thaae

This tiny, beautifully made relief was created for an insurance company. Note the important shadows at the right of the sculpture: these help to counter the flattening effect of the strong colors and deepen the relief.

Remember, powerful colors flatten; light and shade make a piece look much more 3-D.

Hope

36x8x2¹/₂in (90x20x6cm)

Carol Jeanotilla

The artist writes: "I had lost partial use of my hands due to multiple sclerosis and was terrified that I could no longer make my living as an illustrator. This piece was one of my early experiments with a new style, and very much filled me with hope that all was not lost and I could still be an artist. I was right."

In the Gallery

11x16in (28x40cm)
Jill Booth
On one of her many visits to exhibitions, the artist had the idea of creating a relief of two gossiping women, oblivious to the world of art around them. Notice how the bright color and greater relief focus the eye on the foreground figures rather than those in the distance.

Arms of the Baron North

24x17in (60x43cm)

Anthony Gallagher

This elaborate coat of arms was created as an exhibition piece and is constructed from roughly textured watercolor paper, with paper-backed gold foil for the lettering. The artist laboriously cut both supporting beasts individually – instead of cutting through two layers at once, and reversing one – to ensure that both cut edges looked identical. Note the importance of the lighting direction in maximizing the light and shadow effects.

Invicta

39¹/₂x39¹/₂x4in (100x100x10cm)

David Cook

Commissioned by the city of Bruges in Belgium, this coat of arms is technically similar to the *Seal of the City of Philadelphia* (below). However, the pale tones of the heraldic beasts give rise to greater light and shadow effects, so the overall visual impact is more subtle. "Invicta" is the heraldic name for a white horse, rampant. The sculpture is the coat of arms of the County of Kent in England.

Seal of the City of Philadelphia

39¹/₂x39¹/₂x4in (100x100x10cm)

David Cook

Compared with the *Arms of the Baron North* (above), this bold relief uses color to define the shapes, not light and shade, but the result is just as convincing. It was commissioned by a Philadelphia businessman, and after an official tour of Pennsylvania, it was exhibited at a number of historic sites in the US.

Japanese Lady

8x13³/₄in (20x35cm)

Geoff Rayner

This exquisite *blocked* and *layered relief* is derived from an old Japanese woodcut. The shapes were cut with extreme care, but retain a fluency of line that prevents the figure from becoming clumsy. The delicate bending of the edge (compare the *Rose*, p.50) adds to the subtlety of the shading.

Index

Page numbers in *italics* refer to illustrations in Gallery section